# CRAIG V

*The*
*Blond Bomber*

Native Son of Lake Placid

by
**J. Peter Martin**

*To Mike*
*with regards*

*J Peter Martin*

*1941 United States Open &*
*Masters Champion*

I

The Blond Bomber

Sports writers of his day dubbed him The Blond Bomber, not only because of his power and length off the tee, but also because of his natural good looks.

Craig Wood driving on the 16th tee during the opening round of the 40th United States Open held at the Baltusrol Golf Club in New Jersey. Wood posted a 71 on the par-72 course in the opening round.

# Contents

chapter            page

1. Family History . . . . . . . . . . . . . . . . . . . . . . . . . . . . . 2

2. Growing Up in Lake Placid . . . . . . . . . . . . . . . . . 10
   Exhibitions, Teachers and Caddying

3. College Years and First Club Position . . . . . . . . 29

4. New Jersey Years and Tournament Golf . . . . . . . 32

5. British Open-Major Tournament . . . . . . . . . . . . 39

6. The Masters-Major Tournament . . . . . . . . . . . . 47

7. The P.G.A. - Major Tournament . . . . . . . . . . . . . 60

8. The United States Open - Major Tournament . . 65

9. Hale America . . . . . . . . . . . . . . . . . . . . . . . . . . . 76

10. Ryder Cup . . . . . . . . . . . . . . . . . . . . . . . . . . . . . 80

11. Winged Foot . . . . . . . . . . . . . . . . . . . . . . . . . . . 84

12. Dunlop Tire & Rubber Company . . . . . . . . . . . 88

13. Lake Placid - . . . . . . . . . . . . . . . . . . . . . . . . . . . 95
    Craig Wood Golf Course & Exhibitions

14. Indian Lodge Hunting Camp . . . . . . . . . . . . . . 116

15. Lucaya Resort - Grand Bahamas . . . . . . . . . . . 121

16. Back Home and Laid to Rest, Lake Placid . . . . . 125

## Preface

Growing up and caddying in the Adirondacks as a young boy, and later becoming the golf professional at the Whiteface Club in Lake Placid, New York, I became fascinated with the colorful golf history associated with the area. After writing Adirondack Golf Courses Past & Present, I decided next to honor one of our hometown heroes, professional golfer Craig Wood and chronicle his deeds.

The purpose of this book was to offer a glimpse of what golf was like in Lake Placid when Wood was growing up, then follow his illustrious and colorful career, including the major golf tournaments he played in and later his association with his home town where the course was named in his honor.

Once again it is hoped that the descriptions and photographs will prove of interest to golfers and non-golfers alike. My gratitude to all who have helped me in this endeavor, for any errors in my efforts, my heartfelt apology.

## Acknowledgments

My special thanks to : Annoel Krider, my wife, Pat Martin, my
father, Jack Shea, Olympic gold medal speed skater and long
time friend of Craig Wood, Mary McKenzie, Lake Placid,
North Elba historian, Laura Viscome, Lake Placid News
correspondent, Ray Randall, long time friend of Craig Wood,
Ray LaGoy, PGA golf professional and friend of Wood, Joe
Tomlinson, editor & publisher of New Jersey Golf & Travel
Journal, Rand Jerris Ph.D, Librarian & Historian U.S.G.A.,
Douglas Ladue Smith, Winged Foot historian, Bruce & Louis
LeClaire, Craig Wood's cousins, Ken Torrance, family friend,
Kathleen Bigrows, Barbara & Charles Kelly, Phil Kessler, Jeff
Gronauer, Mike Treska, Guido Cribari, Virginia Wood Powers
& Scott Wood, sister & brother of Craig Wood, Craig Wood
Golf Professionals: Brian Halpenny, Ed Kriel, Joe Delong,
James Wasson, Lynn Wilson, Course Superintendent, Butch
Martin, North Elba Park District Manager, Gary Slatter Golf
Pro, U.S.G.A. Golf Museum & Library, Gail Randall, Barry &
Wilson Printing, layout, Lake Placid Library, New York Public
Library, U.S.G.A. Record Book, Lake Placid News, Lake Placid
Historical Society & Museum.

## Introduction

When people think of Lake Placid, they usually associate it with winter sports. This world renowned village hosted the 1932 and 1980 Winter Olympic Games, the latter providing us with the U.S. hockey team's valiant victory over the Soviet Union leading to a Gold Medal known since as The Miracle on Ice. There is a great history in this small village which has produced well over 100 Olympians and at least as many world class national and international events. Lake Placid is truly the home of champions - past, present and future.

Few people realize, however, that Lake Placid first achieved prominence in the late 1800's as an important summer resort. It was also home to one of the world's greatest golfers: "Craig Wood" born November 18, 1901. As a caddy, Wood learned the game well enough to later win 21 major tournaments, including The Masters and United States Open while setting 28 course records along the way. Wood was also a player who suffered the fate of losing more close finishes in major championships than any player of his time. He lost a playoff for the British Open (the only one he entered) lost in a PGA Championship in extra holes, a Masters in a playoff, and a United States Open in a double playoff.

But he did, however, give tournament golf a touch of class in its formative years, for in golf, winning graciously and losing with equal grace are indeed the marks of a winner. He further distinguished himself in his celebrated career by playing on three Ryder Cup teams. His last tournament victory was The Canadian Open (1942). Three years later he retired from competitive golf and subsequently was elected to the Professional Golfers' Hall of Fame.

# Craig Wood - Native Son of Lake Placid

When Wood was a young boy there was a great deal of interest being created in the game of golf. Golf, called the sport of kings, had been brought to America from Scotland and by the turn of the century it had been discovered by the rich in America.

Nowhere was this more evident then in Lake Placid, New York which had come into prominence as a fashionable summer resort with no less then seven golf courses in the small alpine village.

Wealthy families from the northeastern cities found the clean, cool and clear Adirondack mountain air to their liking and began to spend entire summers in the region.

Arriving for the season these families would stay in rustic and luxurious private camps or in the many grand hotels such as the Lake Placid Club, Stevens Hotel, Ruisseaumont or the Whiteface Inn built on the shores of Mirror Lake or Lake Placid.

Needless to say the degree of success of the hotels was greatly enhanced by the proximity of a golf course nearby and Lake Placid by the turn of the century had become the perfect summer paradise and golfing destination.

Craig Wood was quite fortunate to have grown up in that era and to have had the perfect summer job, a "caddy." By working at the local courses he had the opportunity to associate with the leading Scottish teaching professionals of the day and also able to watch and witness the many golf exhibitions featuring world class players. It was a great environment in which to learn to play the game and by the age of 16 he was a scratch player.

What Lake Placid did for Wood is difficult to assess, but one thing was for sure, it served the native son well by shaping his game, his life and his illustrious golfing career.

On November 18, 1901 Charles Ralph Wood
was born in Lake Placid, New York, the son of
Charles and Gertrude Mooney Wood. He changed his
name to Craig Wood when he turned professional.

*Lake Placid
is where
Craig Wood
learned the
game.*

Lake Placid, New York may seem an unlikely place for a golf pro like Craig Wood to grow up, but there is a rich and colorful history of golf associated with the small alpine village.

The Wood homestead was set deep in the forested wilderness high peak region of the Adirondacks. This unspoiled mountain area was home to numerous lakes, ponds, rivers, and brooks.

Also nearby, was a trail which led to Mt. Marcy, once called Tahawus, and Indian name meaning "the cloud splitter," the highest peak in New York State standing 5,344 feet above sea level.

Photo taken across road from Homestead

# Family History

Craig Wood's roots in the Lake Placid North Elba District run deep with both his grandfather and great grandfather being Adirondack pioneers and area settlers.

Craig Wood's great grandfather, Milo Wood, came from Vermont as a young man and settled in Port Henry, New York in the early 1800's. He was actively engaged in mercantile pursuits, when in1848 in the prime of his life, he passed away leaving his widow Harriet Farrington Wood and their three sons Isaac, Jacob and Charles. She married again to Harvey Smith of Westport, New York, by whom she had one son named Walter who died at the age of fifteen. She (Harriet) died in 1894 at the age of seventy-seven.

On his father's death, Jacob K. Wood, born April 17, 1845, went to live with his uncle Robert G. Scott, a farmer in North Elba. Scott had come with his family from Keene, New Hampshire and had become a successful farmer.

After the deaths of his uncle and aunt, Jacob Wood, a young farmer himself, inherited a share of the Scott property which amounted to fourteen hundred dollars.

In June 1867 Mr. Wood was united in marriage to Amelia Mooney. She was born in Croton on the Hudson in 1846, daughter of Thomas and Anne (Toomey) Mooney.

Photo Bruce LeClaire

Thomas Mooney, who was a native of Ireland and a carpenter by trade, emigrated to America in young manhood and settled in Croton, but later moved to Keene, where he died in 1879, aged seventy-five years. He married Anne Toomey, a native of England, and had a family of fifteen children. With the single exception of a few months spent in Springfield, Jacob Wood continued to reside in North Elba, where he carried on general farming. Besides his homestead property, which contained one hundred and sixty acres, he owned a tract of land approximately three hundred and twenty-two acres. The farm was situated upon the road leading to Adirondack Loj, and he supplied that particular resort with farm products. Formerly he took summer boarders, who found his pleasant home and healthy surroundings a quiet and agreeable retreat in which to enjoy an outing during the heated term.

The farm was called The Holly House and later to be called The Wood's Boarding House. It would soon become a famous spot in its own right for fishermen and hunters.

"Mr. Jacob Wood was not only a successful farmer, but a natural woodsman. He was an enthusiastic hunter, and had shot many deer and foxes. His opinion on matters pertaining to hunting was often sought, and he has frequently been quoted in "Forest and Stream", the leading American authority on fish and game. He was a man of great stature, being nearly six and a half feet tall, and of Herculean strength. His unflagging industry brought him fairly good returns, and as a man of strict business habits he quietly accumulated property.

Mr. & Mrs. Wood had four sons and two daughters. Of these, Walter S. and William R. were merchants in Lake Placid. Charles H., Ira, Hattie and Edith lived at home. Jacob was liberal-minded and of strict integrity, and during life he was a friend of the poor and needy. In the year 1896 he died at home of pneumonia. At the time he was one of North Elba's most respected and beloved citizens. In the Elizabeth (N.Y.) Post of February 20, 1896, from which the above extract has been taken, appears the following tribute to his personal character.

"At home with his family he was all that affection could claim. He was kind and considerate and faithful to the utmost degree. We have often enjoyed the hospitality of his roof, and know how well he loved fun, and how exceedingly humorous he was at times. Having known him long and intimately, we do not hesitate to say that we never met a truer or more manly man than Jacob K. Wood. He lived to see the wilderness blossom like the rose, and has gone to the grave in the fifty-first year of his age, generally lamented by all who knew him."

In politics Mr. Wood was a Democrat. His decease deprived the town of an esteemed and valued citizen, and his children of a fond father, who spared nothing to furnish them with all the advantages necessary to make them good and useful members of the community.

The following research was written in 1983 by Virginia Wood Powers, Craig Wood's sister and given to the author by Bruce & Lewis LeClaire, cousins of Craig Wood.

Craig Wood's father, Charles Wood, who was born in Lake Placid in 1872, married Gertrude Mooney and had five children: Joan, Margaret, Raymond, Scott and Craig. He was a forester for the J.J. Rogers Company, their chief timber cruiser and overall outdoor superintendent of their lumbering operations, in fact making the first known ascent of Mt. Phelps in 1904 while measuring timber to be felled.

He was a big man at six feet eight inches tall and weighed about 275 pounds. He was broad shouldered, and narrow of the waist and was considered to be one of the strongest men to have ever lived in the Adirondack Mountains.

In his spare time he was also a very popular guide and guided for Professor Charles E. Peck, state botanist, during his 1893 survey of North Elba and Adirondack plants. The two were also the first to make a recorded ascent of Wright Peak in 1893. He also guided for Henry Van Hoevenberg, builder of the original Adirondack Loj.

He was held in high regard by the Lake Placid community, not only for his tremendous physical capacity, but also for his compassion and regard for others. Mary MacKenzie, the North Elba Town Historian who knew Charles Wood said,

*"he was one of the finest, most handsome, most memorable men I had ever met in my lifetime."*

Charles Wood headed the pulp drive every year
for the Rogers Company. Although the process was
dangerous, with many log jams, it was the most
economical way to get the logs to the mill. It was said
that he saved many a man from drowning on the river
drives.

*Road to Adirondack Loj*

Charles Wood owned large tracts of land in the Lake Placid area, including 500 acres on the Adirondack Loj road where the Wood Boarding House was located.

# Growing Up

*Caddies*

Wood first started caddying at the Ruisseaumont
Hotel Golf Course located on Old Military Road in
Lake Placid. The course, which was built in 1910, was
very popular but also quite unusual in the fact that it
only had fifteen holes.

*Ruissseaumont, Lake Placid*

Ruisseaumont Hotel on Lake Placid burned in 1909.
The golf course was located a few miles away
on Riki Hill.

*Caddy at seventh-hole at Whiteface Inn course in Lake Placid with Whiteface Mt. in the background.*

With the large number of courses in Lake Placid there was a great demand for caddies. It was good money but hard work lugging the large leather bags, especially when some players carried upwards of twenty-five clubs. However, some of the best American golfers in the next few years would come from the caddy ranks, including Wood himself.

Each course had from twenty to thirty caddies. Caddies have been an important part of the game since the 15th century. There was never a better summer job and many of the young caddies, like Wood, graduated to the role of professional golfer.

D. Warren Boyer

Lake Placid Club Course

13

*Stevens Hotel Golf Course, Adirondack Mountains,*
*Lake Placid, New York, 1904*

In his early years he learned many valuable lessons watching and observing not only the members' golf swings but their overall social conduct as well. These were lessons that would serve him well in later years.

*"Mirror Lake" Turning south over two roads, we come to the sixth green on the shore of Mirror Lake, 396 yards.*

*Spacious New Porte Cochere - Stevens Hotel*       *A Putting Contest*

Before the turn of the century the golfing wave was beginning to sweep through the country, becoming the sport of American society. Nowhere was this more evident than in Lake Placid, which was to become the perfect summer paradise and golfing destination.

~~~~~

The Stevens Hotel Golf Course, which was often referred to as the Lake Placid Golf Course, was laid out over Signal Hill in the village, between picturesque Mirror Lake and Lake Placid.

This course was not to be confused with the Lake Placid Club golf course

*Clock golf on the putting green was quite popular & well attended.*

*Lake Placid Club*

*Saturday putting and approaching contest on the 18th green*

The Lake Placid Club was one of the largest golf complexes in the
world at the time with two eighteen hole courses
and two nine hole courses.

Putting greens were literally at the doorstep of many of the hotels. The Lake Placid Club had two large putting greens which permitted the golfer to choose whether his game that day would be a momentary pleasure or a dawn to dusk devotion.

Lake Placid and Whiteface Mountain from Whiteface Inn. One of 4 putting greens on the Whiteface Inn property. This very large green by the lake was where many evening putting tournaments were held

17

In 1913 when Wood was almost twelve years of age and caddying at the local courses, one of the most dramatic episodes in the history of the game occurred when a twenty-year old caddy by the name of Francis Ouimet won the United States Open that was held at Brookline C.C. in Massachusetts. The young Ouimet in a stunning upset had beaten world class British professionals, Ted Ray and Harry Vardon, in a sensational playoff.

All over America it was front page news and every young caddie now carried with him the dream of one day winning the U.S. Open. For Wood, the seed was planted.

*Ouimet, the 1913 United States Open Champion*

Lake Placid Club Boyer Photo

When Wood was in his teens, his game improved dramatically. He now loved the game so much that he even built a small course of his own with the help of his older brother Scott.

The course was located on a large farm on the Averyville Road that his father co-owned with Ola Alford. The boys literally had the run of the farm and the course, which included a pond and an area of about twenty acres. The pond today is called Alford Pond and the farm is owned by Dr. George Hart.

Craig and Scott both respected each others' golfing ability and spent a good amount of time playing and practicing on their private course. There was a great deal of friendly sibling rivalry between them. Some say Scott was as good a golfer as Craig and he helped his younger brother with his swing throughout his career. Scott, however, after having had a taste of city life, decided he would never leave the mountains he loved so much. He preferred the woods and lived in a more reclusive manner.

Their father, Charles Wood, however, made sure the boys' chores came first, when they were growing up. One of their particular responsibilities, both at the farm and hunting camp, was the chopping down of trees and the splitting of firewood.

Their father Charles, a professional woodsman, taught them how to keep their balance and their eyes on the target when swinging the sharp axe. He made sure that they thoroughly understood that simple lesson. It would serve Craig well in later years for there was a remarkable analogy between the way a woodsman swings an axe, generating tremendous speed, and the manner in which a golfer strikes the ball.

At the time, hotels such as the Lake Placid Club, Stevens Hotel, and Whiteface Inn employed some of the best known professional golf instructors in the world.

*Driving contests were also quite prevalent and popular.*
*Seymour Dunn driving at Lake Placid Club Course*

Many of the instructors at the Lake Placid courses were transplanted Scots like John Duncan Dunn, the pro at the Stevens Hotel and his brother Seymour Dunn, director of golf at the Lake Placid Club. They were nephews of Willie Dunn, the famous Scotsman who won the 1894 first unofficial American Open Championship. Their mother, Elizabeth Gourlay, was also the best woman golfer in the world for 21 years. Both were well known and sought after teachers throughout the world. One of Seymour Dunn's best known pupils was Gene Sarazen.

A PRACTICE COURT

Expect to improve and you will improve, but remember the old saying, *nihil sine labore*. Bad golf is often an error of the mind.

Seymour Dunn, the golf director of the Lake
Placid Club from 1908 to 1929, demonstrating the
importance of a steady head. He was an excellent
player, club maker, architect, and author of several
books. Dunn also had eight children, all of whom
were golf professionals at one time or another.

The caliber of play in Lake Placid was quite high
when Wood was growing up and without a doubt
Dunn was a great influence in his golfing career.

*Walter Hagen and Bobby Jones playing in an exhibition match at the Stevens Hotel in Lake Placid. The two were responsible for transporting tournament golf to a spectator sport with large galleries.*

All the nation's leading shotmakers played at the many Lake Placid courses at one time or another. There were numerous exhibitions staged with world class players participating.

Bobby Jones putting on the Stevens Hotel
Course in Lake Placid. Jones was destined for golfing
greatness and won thirteen major championships. He
retired from competitive golf at the age of twenty-
eight. After capturing the GRAND SLAM in 1930,
which consisted of the British Amateur, British Open,
U.S. Amateur, and U.S. Open - all with hickory
shafted clubs.

*Walter Hagen, Stevens Hotel - Lake Placid*

Walter Hagen, known as "the Haig," was perhaps one of the greatest and most colorful players ever to play the game. He was also the first professional to charge admission for playing in exhibition matches. He felt there was more money to be made doing that rather than winning a tournament. In fact, after winning one tournament he endorsed the check and then nonchalantly gave it to his caddy.

He always enjoyed Lake Placid's golf courses. He and Craig Wood would soon become competitors and close friends for many years.

His philosophy was, *"don't hurry, don't worry-& be sure to take time to smell the flowers along the way."*

Walter Hagen, four-time British Open Champion, Seymour Dunn, Director of Golf, Frank Godcheaux, Louisiana State Champion, Joe Kirkwood, Austrailian Open Champion and trick shot artist who toured the world giving exhibitions with Hagen.

This was the format of the early days of professional golf where wealthy golf enthusiasts in a resort area such as Lake Placid paid for their performance.

In the morning round of the exhibition Dunn shot 77, Godcheaux 82, Hagen 77, and Kirkwood 78. In the afternoon, Hagen had 72, Kirkwood 75, Godcheaux 75 and Dunn, 78.

*Exhibitions were quite popular in Lake Placid*

# College Years

After graduating from Lake Placid High School, Wood's parents were well enough off financially to send him to Dean Academy, a private preparatory school, in Franklin, Massachusetts. After Dean Academy, he attended Clarkson College in Potsdam, New York, where he also worked part-time as the first golf professional at the local golf course, the Potsdam Town & Country Club.

Because of the severity of North Country winters Wood decided to transfer to Ryder College in New Jersey, where he would have the opportunity to play a much longer season. He realized that the long winters were not conducive to his game and that if he wanted to pursue golf seriously he would have to leave the northern New York area he loved so much. There was no denying that he could play; the only thing holding him back was the weather.

His first job as a club professional was at a nine-hole course in Winchester, Kentucky, where he worked as a bookkeeper in a tobacco warehouse in the off season. He also worked at the Louisville Country Club. After being the runner up in the Kentucky Open, he won the championship in 1925 at the age of 24.

# New Jersey Years

Wood thrived on competition and was beginning to enter as many tournaments as he could. He realized early on that the amount of prize money wasn't very much, unless you placed in the top two or three spots.

Wood was also one of the few golf professionals who had attended college and he knew that if tournament golf didn't work out for him, he could always get a good job with his business education.

In those early days, a professional's primary objective was to make a name for himself in order to obtain a good paying club professional position. It wasn't until 1936, however, that the Professional Golfers' Association hired a tour director, creating the opportunity to make a good living playing tournament golf.

After leaving Kentucky he returned to the New Jersey area, taking various positions as a club professional. In the winters he would travel to the west coast to play on the winter tour, as did many of his fellow pros. He worked at numerous clubs in the state of New Jersey in the years 1927 to 1938, such as Forest Hills, Norwood, Hollywood, and the Cresmont Club. His duties in those days as a club professional included assembling clubs, selling golf balls and giving lessons. There were also the added responsibilities of greens keeping and managing the club. The pros of that era surely did not have the status of the golf professionals of today and were thus treated somewhat as second class citizens.

In 1929, while he was the professional at the Forest Hills Club in New Jersey, he took a train across the country to Los Angeles and worked his way over to Hawaii on an ocean liner, where he proceeded to win the Hawaiian Open.

Syracuse <u>Post Standard</u>
November 24,1929

## HAWAII GOLF TITLE WON BY
## LAKE PLACID BOY
### Craig Wood Adds Further Laurel to Record

Lake Placid, Nov. 23, –

Craig Wood, son of Mr. & Mrs. Charles Wood of this village, won the open golf championship of Hawaii in a tournament at Honolulu. The final round was played last Sunday. The purse for first place was $1,500.

Wood downed Horton Smith of Joplin, Mo. in the final with a card of 289. Smith shot a 292. Billy Burke of the Westport, N.Y. club was third with a 293.

Wood learned his golf on local courses and is credited with being one of the finest golfers ever turned out in the Adirondacks. He is now professional at the Forest Hills Club, Bloomfield, N.J.

Several weeks ago he took first honors in the Oklahoma City open.

Although Wood would be known throughout the world as one of the longest drivers of the golf ball, he was also known as one of the straightest.

A few years earlier in his career he had a terrific hook but his friend and fellow professional, Wild Bill Mehlhorn, convinced him that if he wanted to compete and win on tour he would have to learn to fade the ball.

He then began doing so with a two-wood (Brassie) instead of the driver. His swing, although flat and somewhat closed at the top, was very powerful. With his new swing not only was Wood winning long drive contests, but in 1933 he was the leading money winner on the winter tour.

Wood also became one of the best putters after he abandoned his old crouch style and changed to a more upright stance over the ball. After that posture change, some of his fellow pros thought him to be a brilliant putter. His putting stroke would come to his rescue more than once in winning tournaments.

During his time in New Jersey he also won the New Jersey Professional Golfers' Association Championship four times. These wins occurred at the Forest Hill Club in Bloomfield in 1928, again in 1930 at the Cresmont Country Club in West Orange, in 1932 at Hopewell Valley Club and in 1938 at Suburban G.C. in Union, New Jersey. He also won the New Jersey Open in 1934 at Braidburn (now Brook Lake C.C.) in Florham Park.

Other notable moments in his New Jersey years included shooting a 69 in the morning round and 71 in the afternoon at the Pine Valley Golf Course. It was a course record which would stand for many years. The highly ranked #1 course was considered by many the most difficult and frightening golf course in the world. It has been called, among other tributes, an examination of golf in the truest sense. He still holds the two-day, seventy-two hole course record of 286 set in 1938.

Perhaps Wood's greatest New Jersey win was when he returned to the Forest Hill Golf Course (where he started his career), and shot an astounding record score of 264, 20 under par, to win the Metropolitan Open. He averaged 66 per round for four rounds, beating Ben Hogan by 11strokes. Hogan was, in those days, the tour's leading money winner and was considered by many to be in a class by himself.

Wood, who was one of New Jersey's greatest golfers, was subsequently inducted into the New Jersey Professional Golfers' Association.

*Wood worked hard on his putting and it certainly paid off. He felt that the one outstanding factor to be remembered is that all putts must be hit firmly, yet the stroke should never be hurried.*

Chalmers Meyers, general manager of the Los Angeles California Open, presenting Craig Wood with his prize winning check after he captured the 1933 Los Angeles Open Tournament. Wood, in fact, batted 1000 on the winter tour by also winning the Pasadena Open and the San Francisco Open.

In the 1930's Wood played against some of the greatest golfers of the day such as Sam Snead, Ben Hogan and Byron Nelson. It was indeed the golden age for American golf.

From archives of Notown Communications

# British Open,

## St. Andrews, Scotland

Craig Wood loses playoff to Densmore Shute

The British Open, known as "The Open," was first played in 1860 at the Prestwick Golf Club. The winner that year was Willie Park, Sr. with a score of 174. Park won the right to wear the championship belt for a year and the bragging rights associated with it. The British Open is a major tournament which is always played on a links course, with the elements of nature always providing a good test of golf.

*Prestwick, a fishing village on the west coast of Scotland*

The British Open is the oldest golf
championship in the world.

Over the next seventy-five years, the number of entrants to the championship increased and finally, in the 1920's, a regional qualifier was added. It was the era when the best American golfers started to cross the Atlantic and compete in the championship.

With players entering from around the world, such as Bobby Jones and Walter Hagen, the tournament was rapidly gaining international status.

In 1933 Wood took an ocean liner to Scotland to play in his first Open. It was held that year at the Royal and Ancient Golf Club of St. Andrews. St. Andrews, (formally founded on May 14, 1754) was a course created by Mother Nature and all the great names in the history of golf have played it at one time or another.

There is no telling when golf first began at St. Andrews, which is often referred to as "the Old Course," but the earliest reference and written evidence places the date around the late 1500's. Needless to say, there is a great deal of history associated with the course.

Wood, after his trip abroad, had to play the customary qualifying round. Not having the opportunity to become familiar with the course, he shot an 82. However, playing the next eighteen holes, he avoided his previous mistakes and qualified by four strokes. During the Open itself he shot 77, 72, 68 and 75. He finished with a total score of 292, tying Densmore Shute for the lead.

On the first hole of the 36-hole playoff with Shute, Wood put his second shot into the Swilcan Burn and chose to remove his shoes and socks to play the ball from the water. According to golf writer Herbert Warren Wind, in his book, The Story of American Golf, "the wisdom of resorting to such desperate measures with thirty five holes left to go in the playoff, was open to question, particularly when Wood, for all his pains, was not able to do better than six, which perhaps cost him the outright victory. He dropped two strokes on that hole, two more on the second hole and after that there was not much to choose between Wood and Shute, with Shute winning by five strokes."

Although Wood lost the tournament, getting his first taste of being a runner up, he is best remembered for the remarkable and much discussed drive at the long fifth hole - Hole O'Cross (out), a par five.

As Bernard Darwin, the golf writer, wrote, "he drove his ball from the tee into one of the bunkers known as 'spectacle' in front of the green. The hole as played that day was 530 yards long and the ball soared up 100 yards from the hole, that this happened, there is no shadow of a doubt, as to how it happened, I give up." It was the longest drive ever seen on the Old Course.

Densmore Shute being congratulated by Craig
Wood immediately after defeating his fellow
countryman in the playoff in the British Open
Championship. Andrew Kirkaldy, Honorary
Professional to the Royal and Ancient is shown on
the left.

"Hell Bunker" where defending British Open champion, Gene Sarazen, lost his chance to win the 1933 Open by taking an eight after hitting a shot into the dreaded bunker to finish one stroke behind.

Bunkers (where sheep once lived) played a major part in the outcome of many an Open at St. Andrews.

In his era, Wood was by far the most powerful and longest driver of the golf ball. In the pubs of St. Andrew's, his name and length off the tees are still talked about.

An eloquent tribute to the long driving Wood is paid to him at the St. Andrews Course, where there is a sign which the Scots put up and still stands, "Craig Wood drove here."

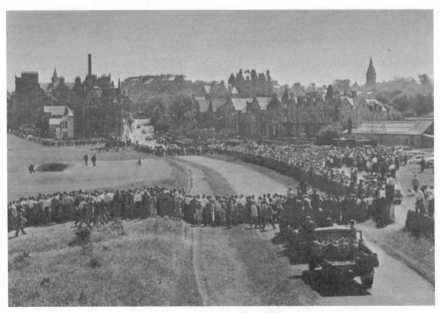

*The Road hole at legendary Old Course*

*Wood receiving a kiss from his wife Jacqueline. Also shown in photo is*
*<u>Rexe</u> their toy pinscher.*

Craig Wood married Jacqueline Valentine, a wealthy New York socialite, in April 1934 just before playing in The Masters in Augusta, Georgia. They lived in the Park Lane Hotel in New York City, where they kept an apartment and garage for his sleek, two-seat, canvas top, 12-cylinder Packard with its exterior luggage racks to carry his golf clubs.

He was a dashing figure in the social life of New York City. His wardrobe consisted of the finest silk ties, cashmere coats, tailored slacks and custom made leather shoes. The handsome Wood was constantly being compared to Hollywood's leading men of that era.

# The Masters

Historic Golf Print

*Augusta National Golf House*

In 1934 the immortal Bobby Jones organized a tournament in Augusta, Georgia called the Augusta Invitational, later to be known simply as the "Masters," played every year in April at the Augusta National Golf Course.

Jones hired and assisted Alister Mackenzie, one of the best known architects of his day, to create one of the most beautiful, most recognizable and revered golf courses anywhere in the world.

The Augusta Club is symbolic of everything good in the game of golf and no course is more immaculately attended or beautiful.

Jones then invited both the best professional and amateur golfers to Augusta, based on qualifications he devised and getting an invitation to play was dearly cherished.

Wood, who was thirty-three years old at the time, received his invitation to play in the glamorous event and after rounds of 71, 74, 69 and 71 felt that he was going to be the eventual winner of the first Augusta invitational. Horton Smith, however, one of the greatest putters in the game, rallied to win the 1934 U.S. Masters in its first year by one stroke with Wood finishing second.

Horton Smith, known as the "Joplin Ghost" from Missouri and one of the game's greatest putters, putting on the eighth green during the first Masters Invitational Golf Tournament at Augusta, Georgia.

Both Smith and Wood were very popular with the gallery because of their taste in clothing, their good looks and overall charm.

*"In the club house at Augusta"*

Bobby Jones shown shaking hands with Craig Wood. Jones retired at the age of twenty-eight from competitive golf except for a couple tournaments, including the Masters. In 1930, Jones won the British Amateur, British Open, U.S. Open, and U.S. Amateur for the Grand Slam, one of the most remarkable feats by one of the greatest golfers of all time.

In 1935 at the second Masters tournament, Wood, who had been playing sensational golf, was in the clubhouse after posting rounds of 69, 72, 68 and 73 for a 282, four-day total. He had played the final eight holes in four under par and once again felt that this was his year and this tournament to win. In fact, he was being congratulated by the organizers, sports writers and his fellow professionals for his soon to be victory.

However, the victor was still out on the course where one of the most famous golf shots ever played occurred on the par-5, fifteenth hole by Gene Sarazen. Having hit his Wilson four wood (Turf Rider), second shot, he watched it go 220 yards over water in front of the green and into the hole for a "double eagle" two.

It was without a doubt, one of the most famous and sensational shots ever played in tournament golf. Receiving maximum publicity and talked about for years to come, it was referred to as "the Shot Heard Around the World."

*Augusta National*

*Sarazen and Wood Signing Scorecards*

The Double Eagle would bring instant fame to
both the tournament and Sarazen himself. What he
had done in fact was to go three under par on one
hole alone to tie Wood, who was in the clubhouse,
still receiving congratulatory handshakes. He then
proceeded to par the last three holes after two putting
the eighteenth, "two of the most difficult putts," he
said later, "that I ever had to make."

With Wood and Sarazen now tied, a 36-hole
playoff was scheduled for the next day (the only one
in Masters history).

*Craig Wood and Gene Sarazen putting in 1935 Masters at Augusta*

Wood, who thought once again that this was his tournament to win, found the playoff to be very difficult both physically and emotionally. In the playoff, he shot 75 on a cold, wet morning, while Sarazen shot 71. In the afternoon round, Wood shot a 74 while Sarazen posted a 73, losing the playoff and the tournament by five strokes. For the second year in a row Craig Wood had finished second.

Unfortunately, Wood was beginning to be called "the number two wood" by the sportswriters for his heartbreaking second place finishes.

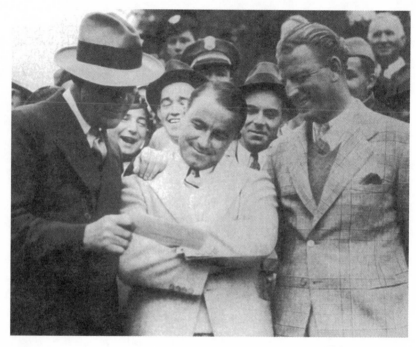

Wood received $800 for his second place finish and another $50 for the thirty six hole playoff. Sarazen was presented his first check of $1,500 from Grantland Rice, the golf writer. Coincidentally, Sarazen had caddied as a young boy for Rice.

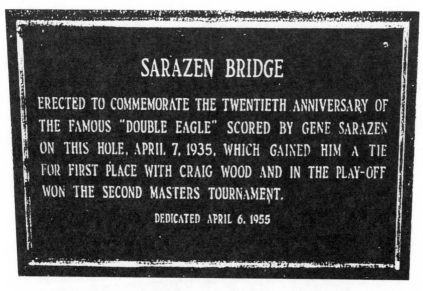

**SARAZEN BRIDGE**

ERECTED TO COMMEMORATE THE TWENTIETH ANNIVERSARY OF
THE FAMOUS "DOUBLE EAGLE" SCORED BY GENE SARAZEN
ON THIS HOLE, APRIL 7, 1935, WHICH GAINED HIM A TIE
FOR FIRST PLACE WITH CRAIG WOOD AND IN THE PLAY-OFF
WON THE SECOND MASTERS TOURNAMENT.

DEDICATED APRIL 6, 1955

The Sarazen Bridge over the pond on the fifteenth hole was dedicated in 1955 on the twentieth anniversary of the famed double eagle. Both Sarazen and Wood attended the ceremony.

Sarazen also invented the sand wedge which revolutionized the game. A great player, he won four major championships, including two U.S. Opens, three PGAs, a Masters and the British Open.

**1934**

| Horton Smith | 70 | 72 | 70 | 72 | 282 |
| Craig Wood | 71 | 74 | 69 | 71 | 285 |
| Billy Burke | 72 | 71 | 70 | 73 | 286 |
| Paul Runyan | 74 | 71 | 70 | 71 | 286 |

**1935**

| Gene Sarazen | 68 | 71 | 73 | 70 | 282 |
| Craig Wood | 69 | 72 | 68 | 73 | 282 |
| (Sarazen won play-off 144 to 149) | | | | | |
| Olin Dutra | 70 | 70 | 70 | 74 | 284 |

In the 1936 Masters, Wood shot an 88 in the first round of the tournament, but came back the next day with a 67, making up 21 strokes from the previous day. However, with two rounds to go, he had too much ground to make up on Horton Smith, the eventual winner.

Finally, in 1941, Wood, who had been one of the most consistent hard luck golfers, would win his first major tournament, "The Masters."

Historic Golf Print

He started the day with a magnificent 66, five strokes better than any other golfer in the field. It was to be his best start and his best chance to change his image of being the perennial runner up (The Number Two Wood, to which he was often referred.)

Herbert Warren Wind, the great golf writer, wrote "that no tournament gallery ever pulled harder than that gallery did for him as did golfing fans throughout the world."

Wood shot 71 the second day and 71 the third day. On the fourth and final day, with nine holes to go, he had lost his lead and was tied with Byron Nelson.

Wood, however, was not to be denied this time shooting 34 on the back nine holes to Nelson's 37, thus winning by three strokes. At 39 years of age he had erased his runner up image and was finally The Masters champion.

**1941**

| | | | | | |
|---|---|---|---|---|---|
| Craig Wood | 66 | 71 | 71 | 72 | 280 |
| Byron Nelson | 71 | 69 | 73 | 70 | 283 |
| Sam Byrd | 73 | 70 | 68 | 74 | 285 |

**Past Masters Champions Honored in 1953**

(left to right) Nelson, Demaret, Picard, Smith, Hogan, Wood, Harmon, Sarazen and Snead

Historic Golf Print

**1934**

# Professional Golfers' Association Championship
## Buffalo, New York

Craig Wood loses to Paul Runyan
in sudden death playoff

The Professional Golf Championship first played in 1916 is one of the four major championships comprising the modern "Grand Slam."

It is also the flagship event for all the members of the Professional Golfers' Association of America.

It had been traditionally a match play event where two rounds a day were played. In 1958 it was changed to medal (stroke play). This change was necessitated by the growing popularity of the game and also because of increased television coverage.

In 1934 the Professional Golfers' Association Championship was held at the Park Country Club in Buffalo, New York. Following the final thirty six holes of match play, Craig Wood and Paul Runyan were tied. The match had been squared eight times and although Wood's powerful long drives gave him an advantage, Runyan's precision short game more than made up for it. They continued playing until the 38th hole, where Wood lost the tournament to Runyan, nicknamed "Little Poison" because of his deadly accuracy, especially his putter, which killed off many an opponent.

Ironically, Runyan said that if Wood hadn't taken the interest in him as a young player, convincing him of his talent and hiring him as his assistant in 1930 at the Forest Hill Club in New Jersey, he probably wouldn't have won the tournament. Runyan said that "Wood had the coolest demeanor of anybody I've ever seen. He was a great friend and mentor."

*The new professional champion, Paul Runyan (left), being presented with the trophy by George Jacobus, President of the P.G.A. (right) winning the title July 29 at Buffalo, N.Y. Craig Wood of Hollywood, N.J., the runner-up, is shown between the pair.*

In the days of match play, stymies often occurred and had a great influence on the results. A stymie was when your opponent's ball was lying on the green between your ball and the hole. At this point you were required to chip over it. The rule was abolished in 1951.

# The United States Open

The United States Open, also known as the National Open, is the oldest and most important championship in the United States.

The first Open was played on October 4, 1895 in Newport, Rhode Island with a field of eleven. They played the nine-hole course four times with Horace Rawlins eventually winning the $150 first prize.

In 1913, after the Europeans had dominated the tournament for so many years, a virtually unknown young American caddy, by the name of Francis Ouimet, defeated the British professionals Harry Vardon and Ted Ray in a playoff at the country club in Brookline, Massachusetts. It would be the beginning of American dominance in the pursuit of a United States Open title.

Craig Wood knew how important it would be to win the Open and played in many of them. His first was in 1925 at the age of twenty four when he tied for fifty second. In 1928 he tied for forty sixth place and in 1930 tied for 9th.

In 1933 Wood, the leading money winner on the winter tour, was playing well and on top of his game. The 1933 Open was held at the North Shore Country Club in Illinois where he took third place, three strokes back of the winner, Johnny Goodman.

The next year would be a major turning point in his golfing career, winning the Galveston Open, tying for second place in both the Texas Open and the Charleston Open, and being runner up in the Masters.

He was winning tournaments but it was the United States Open title he so coveted that remained elusive.

Winged Foot Golf Club

# United States Open
# Philadelphia Country Club
Pennsylvania

**1939**

The 1939 U.S. Open was held at the Philadelphia Country Club in West Conshohocken, Pennsylvania and Wood after rounds of 70, 71, and 72 was tied for the lead with Byron Nelson and Densmore Shute. During the eighteen hole playoff an unfortunate incident occurred coming into the finishing hole when Wood hooked his tee shot, hitting a spectator and knocking him unconscious. The man was carried off the course with no serious injuries. However, Wood was quite shaken and upset, though he somehow managed to hit his next shot onto the green a few feet from the hole. All he had to do then was to sink the putt to win the United States Open. He left it an inch short of the hole, while Nelson proceeded to make his putt for a birdie and a tie.

In the playoff Shute was eliminated with a 76 while Nelson and Wood, who had both shot 68 had to play another eighteen holes to decide the championship.

During the playoff Nelson was in great form, sinking his second shot on the par 4, 453-yard fourth hole using a one iron, one of the most difficult clubs to hit. He called it one of the greatest shots he had ever made in his life. After his eagle two the momentum was with Nelson, and Wood never had a chance to catch him, losing the playoff by three shots, 70 to 73.

Craig Wood, by losing another playoff, was fast becoming the game's unluckiest golfer.

*Philadelphia. Craig Wood changes to street clothes in club house of the*
*Spring Mill course. A playoff will decide the National Open*
*Championship which he hopes to win.*

## 1939
## FORTY-THIRD OPEN CHAMPIONSHIP

Held at Philadelphia Country Club, (Spring Mill Course), West Conshohocken, Pa., June 8–10.
Yardage—6,786.    Par 69.    1,193 Entries; 165 Starters.

64 Contestants who completed 72 holes.

| | | | | | | Score | Money Prize |
|---|---|---|---|---|---|---|---|
| 1 | Byron Nelson, Reading C.C., Pa. | 72 | 73 | 71 | 68 | 284 | $1,000.00 |
| 2 | Craig Wood, Winged Foot G.C., N.Y. | 70 | 71 | 71 | 72 | 284 | 800.00 |
| 3 | Denny Shute, Huntington, W.Va., | 70 | 72 | 70 | 72 | 284 | 700.00 |
| 4 | *Marvin (Bud) Ward, Spokane, C.C., Wash. | 69 | 73 | 71 | 72 | 285 | MEDAL |
| 5 | Sam Snead, Greenbrier, G. & T. C., W. Va. | 68 | 71 | 73 | 74 | 286 | 600.00 |
| 6 | Johnny Bulla, Chicago, III. | 72 | 71 | 68 | 76 | 287 | 450.00 |
| 7 | Ralph Guldahl, Braidburn C.C., N.J. | 71 | 73 | 72 | 72 | 288 | 325.00 |
| | Dick Metz, Mill Road Farm G.C., III. | 76 | 72 | 71 | 69 | 288 | 325.00 |
| 9 | Ky Laffoon, Northmoor C.C., III. | 76 | 70 | 73 | 70 | 289 | 175.00 |
| | Harold L. McSpaden, Winchester C.C., Mass. | 70 | 73 | 71 | 75 | 289 | 175.00 |
| | Paul Runyan, Metropolis, C.C., N.Y. | 76 | 70 | 71 | 72 | 289 | 175.00 |
| 12 | Harry E. Cooper, Shenecossett C.C., Conn. | 71 | 72 | 75 | 72 | 290 | 108.33 |
| | Ed Dudley, Philadelphia Country C., Pa. | 76 | 72 | 73 | 69 | 290 | 108.34 |
| | Henry G. Picard, Hershey C.C., Pa. | 72 | 72 | 72 | 74 | 290 | 108.33 |
| 15 | Horton Smith, Oak Park C.C., III. | 72 | 68 | 75 | 76 | 291 | 100.00 |
| 16 | Sam Byrd, Philadelphia Country C., Pa. | 75 | 71 | 72 | 74 | 292 | 66.67 |
| | Olin Dutra, Wilshire C.C., Calif. | 70 | 74 | 70 | 78 | 292 | 66.67 |
| | Clayton Heafner, Charlotte, N.C. | 73 | 73 | 66 | 80 | 292 | 66.66 |
| | *Wilford Wehrle, Racine C.C., Wis. | 71 | 77 | 69 | 75 | 292 | — |
| 20 | Jimmy Hines, Lakeville C., N.Y. | 73 | 74 | 77 | 69 | 293 | 50.00 |
| | John E. Rogers, Denver C.C., Colo. | 75 | 70 | 69 | 79 | 293 | 50.00 |
| 22 | Tommy Armour, Medinah C.C., III. | 70 | 75 | 69 | 80 | 294 | 50.00 |
| | Jimmy Demaret, Brae-Burn C.C., Texas | 72 | 76 | 72 | 74 | 294 | 50.00 |
| | John Revolta, Evanston G.C., III. | 73 | 76 | 71 | 74 | 294 | 50.00 |
| 25 | Robert A. Cruickshank, C.C., of Virginia, Va. | 73 | 74 | 73 | 75 | 295 | 50.00 |
| | Jim Foulis, Ruth Lake C.C., III. | 73 | 75 | 77 | 70 | 295 | 50.00 |
| | E.J. (Dutch) Harrison, Oak Park C.C., III. | 75 | 72 | 74 | 74 | 295 | 50.00 |
| | Matt Kowal, Philmont C.C., Pa. | 69 | 76 | 75 | 75 | 295 | 50.00 |
| 29 | Victor Ghezzi, Deal G.C., N.J. | 73 | 71 | 76 | 76 | 296 | 50.00 |
| | Edward Oliver, Hornell C.C., N.Y. | 75 | 77 | 72 | 72 | 296 | 50.00 |
| | Felix Serafin, C.C., of Scranton, Pa. | 80 | 72 | 71 | 73 | 296 | 50.00 |
| 32 | Al Espinosa, Portage C.C., Ohio | 75 | 73 | 74 | 75 | 297 | 12.50 |
| | Alvin Krueger, Beloit Municipal G.C., Wis. | 71 | 77 | 73 | 76 | 297 | 12.50 |
| | Ray Mangrum, Oakmont, Pa. | 71 | 74 | 81 | 71 | 297 | 12.50 |
| | Jim Turnesa, Louisquisset G.C., R.I. | 75 | 74 | 75 | 73 | 297 | 12.50 |
| 36 | Arthur Bell, Midwick C.C., Calif. | 73 | 75 | 79 | 71 | 298 | |
| | Leo J. Walper, Bethesda, Md. | 74 | 75 | 79 | 70 | 298 | |
| 38 | Terl Johnson, Plymouth C.C., Pa. | 73 | 76 | 76 | 74 | 299 | |
| | Edwin C. Kingsley, C.C., Salt Lake City, Utah | 76 | 75 | 73 | 75 | 299 | |
| | Frank Moore, Mount Washington G.C., N.H. | 73 | 70 | 77 | 79 | 299 | |
| | Sam Parks, Jr., South Hills C.C., Pa. | 73 | 73 | 77 | 76 | 299 | |
| 42 | Billy Burke, C.C., Cleveland Ohio | 74 | 74 | 77 | 75 | 300 | |
| | William A. Francis, Blairmont C.C., Pa. | 78 | 74 | 74 | 74 | 300 | |
| | Gene Kunes, Norristown, Pa. | 76 | 73 | 75 | 76 | 300 | |
| | Lawson Little, Bretton Woods C.C., N.H. | 69 | 74 | 76 | 81 | 300 | |
| | Frank Walsh, Rumson C.C., N.J. | 74 | 75 | 76 | 75 | 300 | |
| 47 | Joe Belfore, C.C. of Detroit, Mich. | 76 | 76 | 68 | 81 | 301 | |
| | *Otto P. Greiner, Rodgers Forge C., Md. | 77 | 73 | 77 | 74 | 301 | |
| | Gene Sarazen, Brookfield, Conn. | 74 | 72 | 79 | 76 | 301 | |
| | Pat Sawyer, Birmingham G.C., Mich. | 75 | 75 | 77 | 74 | 301 | |
| | *William P. Turnesa, Briar Hills G. & C.C., N.Y. | 77 | 74 | 76 | 74 | 301 | |
| 52 | Bruce Coltart, Woodcrest, C.C., N.J. | 78 | 73 | 80 | 71 | 302 | |
| | Tom Creavy, Albany C.C., N.Y. | 72 | 78 | 77 | 75 | 302 | |
| | Al Houghton, Georgetown Prep G.C., Md. | 73 | 76 | 76 | 77 | 302 | |
| 55 | Ted Luther, Churchill Valley C.C., Pa. | 73 | 75 | 77 | 78 | 303 | |
| 56 | Tony Manero, Salem C.C., Mass. | 74 | 76 | 78 | 76 | 304 | |
| | Lloyd Mangrum, Los Angeles, Calif. | 70 | 74 | 81 | 79 | 304 | |
| 58 | Ted Turner, Pine Valley G.C., N.J. | 75 | 74 | 80 | 76 | 305 | |
| 59 | George Von Elm, Taft, Calif. | 72 | 77 | 76 | 81 | 306 | |
| | Norman Von Nida, Sidney, Australia | 79 | 73 | 72 | 82 | 306 | |
| 61 | *Edward L. Meister, Jr., Canterbury G.C., Ohio | 71 | 76 | 81 | 79 | 307 | |
| 62 | Ben Hogan, Century C.C., N.Y. | 76 | 74 | 78 | 80 | 308 | |
| | George Slingerland, Greensboro C.C., N.C. | 74 | 78 | 81 | 75 | 308 | |
| 64 | Frank Gelhot, Ridgewood G.C., Ohio | 74 | 76 | 78 | 81 | 309 | |

*Amateur.
Playoff—June 11-12: Nelson, 68--70--138; Wood, 68--73--141; Shute, 76--eliminated.

## FORTY-FOURTH OPEN CHAMPIONSHIP

Held at Canterbury Golf Club, Cleveland, Ohio, June 6—8.
1,161 Entries; 165 Starters.

58 Contestants who completed 72 holes.

| | | | | | | Score | Money Prize |
|---|---|---|---|---|---|---|---|
| 1 | Lawson Little, Bretton Woods, N.H. | 72 | 69 | 73 | 73 | 287 | $1,000.00 |
| 2 | Gene Sarazen, Brookfield Center, Conn. | 71 | 74 | 70 | 72 | 287 | 800.00 |
| 3 | Horton Smith, Oak Park C.C., Ill. | 69 | 72 | 78 | 69 | 288 | 700.00 |
| 4 | Craig Wood, Winged Foot G.C., N.Y. | 72 | 73 | 72 | 72 | 289 | 600.00 |
| 5 | Ben Hogan, Century C.C., N.Y. | 70 | 73 | 74 | 73 | 290 | 325.00 |
| | Ralph Guldahl, Chicago, Ill. | 73 | 71 | 76 | 70 | 290 | 325.00 |
| | Lloyd Mangrum, Oak Park C.C., Ill. | 75 | 70 | 71 | 74 | 290 | 325.00 |
| | Byron Nelson, Inverness C., Ohio | 72 | 74 | 70 | 74 | 290 | 325.00 |
| 9 | Dick Metz, Oak Park C.C., Ill. | 75 | 72 | 72 | 72 | 291 | 175.00 |
| 10 | Ed Dudley, Philadelphia Country C., Pa. | 73 | 75 | 71 | 73 | 292 | 137.50 |
| | Frank Walsh, Rumson C.C., N.J. | 73 | 69 | 71 | 79 | 292 | 137.50 |
| 12 | Tommy Armour, Medinah C.C., Ill. | 73 | 74 | 75 | 71 | 293 | 100.00 |
| | Harold L. McSpaden, Winchester C.C., Mass. | 74 | 72 | 70 | 77 | 293 | 100.00 |
| | Henry G. Picard, Hershey C.C., Pa. | 73 | 73 | 71 | 76 | 293 | 100.00 |
| 15 | Victor Ghezzi, Deal G.C., N.J. | 70 | 74 | 75 | 75 | 294 | 100.00 |
| 16 | Jim Foulis, Ruth Lake C.C., Ill. | 73 | 73 | 77 | 72 | 295 | 50.00 |
| | Gene Kunes, Holmesburg, C.C., Pa. | 76 | 72 | 73 | 74 | 295 | 50.00 |
| | Johnny Revolta, Evanston G.C., Ill. | 73 | 74 | 72 | 76 | 295 | 50.00 |
| | Sam Snead, Shawnee C.C., Pa. | 67 | 74 | 73 | 81 | 295 | 50.00 |
| 20 | Andrew Gibson, Bonnie View G.C., Md. | 71 | 75 | 77 | 73 | 296 | 50.00 |
| | Jimmy Hines, Lakeville, C., N.Y. | 73 | 74 | 77 | 72 | 296 | 50.00 |
| | Felix Serafin, C.C. of Scranton, Pa. | 77 | 74 | 71 | 74 | 296 | 50.00 |
| 23 | Jock Hutchison, Jr., Forest Hills C.C., Ill. | 73 | 72 | 75 | 77 | 297 | 50.00 |
| | Eddie Kirk, Glen Oaks G.C., Mich. | 73 | 77 | 74 | 73 | 297 | 50.00 |
| | *Wilford Wehrle, Tam O'Shanter C.C., Ill. | 78 | 73 | 72 | 74 | 297 | ——— |
| | Leland J. Wilcox, Sunnyside C.C., Iowa | 75 | 73 | 74 | 75 | 297 | 50.00 |
| 27 | Ray Mangrum, Oakmont, Pa. | 73 | 78 | 75 | 72 | 298 | 50.00 |
| 28 | Johnny Farrell, Baltusrol G.C., N.J. | 75 | 77 | 76 | 71 | 299 | 50.00 |
| 29 | Bruce Coltart, Seaview G.C., N.J. | 80 | 72 | 74 | 74 | 300 | 30.00 |
| | *Jim Ferrier, Sydney, Australia | 73 | 74 | 78 | 75 | 300 | ——— |
| | Al Huske, Kishwaukee C.C., Ill. | 70 | 80 | 76 | 74 | 300 | 30.00 |
| | Sam Parks, Jr., South Hills C.C., Pa. | 69 | 74 | 79 | 78 | 300 | 30.00 |
| | Henry B. Ramson, Glen Garden G. & C.C., Texas | 75 | 77 | 74 | 74 | 300 | 30.00 |
| | Jack Ryan, Louisville C.C., Ky. | 75 | 75 | 77 | 73 | 300 | 30.00 |
| | *Andrew Szwedko, North Park G.C., Pa. | 76 | 77 | 76 | 71 | 300 | ——— |
| 36 | *Richard D. Chapman, Aronimink G.C., Pa. | 74 | 78 | 76 | 73 | 301 | |
| | Willie Goggin, San Francisco, Calif. | 78 | 74 | 75 | 74 | 301 | |
| | Matt Kowal, Philmont C.C., Pa. | 72 | 75 | 77 | 77 | 301 | |
| | Tony Manero, Salem C.C., Mass. | 75 | 75 | 77 | 74 | 301 | |
| | Johnny Morris, C.C. of Tuscaloosa, Ala. | 75 | 77 | 74 | 75 | 301 | |
| 41 | Sam D. Byrd, Merion Cricket C., Pa. | 72 | 78 | 79 | 73 | 302 | |
| 42 | Toney Penna, Dayton, Ohio | 80 | 73 | 76 | 74 | 303 | |
| 43 | Leonard Dodson, Kansas City C.C., Mo. | 72 | 72 | 80 | 81 | 305 | |
| | Al Espinosa, Portage C.C., Ohio | 79 | 71 | 76 | 79 | 305 | |
| | Jim Milward, Blackhawk C.C., Wis. | 74 | 79 | 76 | 76 | 305 | |
| | John Thoren, Woodland G.C., Mass. | 73 | 78 | 77 | 77 | 305 | |
| 47 | Al Brosch, Bethpage State Park, N.Y. | 74 | 73 | 82 | 77 | 306 | |
| | John E. Rogers, Denver C.C., Colo. | 73 | 76 | 79 | 78 | 306 | |
| 49 | Paul Runyan, Metropolis C.C., N.Y. | 74 | 79 | 78 | 76 | 307 | |
| 50 | Jerry Gianferante, Brattleboro C.C., Vt. | 76 | 77 | 81 | 74 | 308 | |
| | Henry J. Kaiser, Meadowbrook G.C., Wis. | 71 | 78 | 80 | 79 | 308 | |
| 52 | *Robert N. Babbish, Brooklands G. & C.C., Mich. | 71 | 77 | 80 | 81 | 309 | |
| | Bill Barbour, Sleepy Hollow C.C., Ohio | 75 | 78 | 80 | 76 | 309 | |
| 54 | Mike Pavella, Washington County G. & C.C., Pa. | 79 | 74 | 81 | 76 | 310 | |
| 55 | Frank Commisso, Irondequoit C.C., N.Y. | 73 | 78 | 80 | 81 | 312 | |
| | Pete Webb, Cleveland Springs G.C., N.C. | 77 | 74 | 83 | 78 | 312 | |
| | Ock Willoweit, Dayton, Ohio | 75 | 78 | 82 | 77 | 312 | |
| 58 | *Toby Lyons, Riverside G.C., Pa. | 77 | 76 | 80 | 80 | 313 | |

Six players were disqualified for beginning their final round ahead of their scheduled
starting time because of threatening weather. Ed (Porky) Oliver was among the six,
and he finished with an unofficial score of 287, which would have tied him with Little
and Sarazen.

Playoff 18 holes, June 9—Little, 70; Sarazen, 73.

*Amateur. Gold medals awarded to Wilford Wehrle, Jim Ferrier and Andrew Szwedko.
Prize money totaling $6,000 awarded to professionals returning scores up to 300, inclusive.

In 1941 the Open was held at the Colonial Club, in Fort Worth, Texas. This was a comparatively new course, having been opened in 1936. Cary Middlecoff called it "the toughest par 70 in the world." Two weeks before the tournament began, however, the Masters Champion suffered a back injury when he happened to sneeze while shaving. This aggravated a prior injury he had suffered earlier in the year when he had fallen heavily in a wet bunker.

Wood suffered excruciating muscle spasms and doctors prescribed a heavy leather corset and harness for him if he decided to play. It was very uncomfortable and restricted his swing. But playing without it would have been quite difficult since the pain was so intense he wouldn't be able to concentrate.

Nonetheless, he proceeded to play in the Open, being careful not to twist the wrong way, placing himself out of contention. On the very first hole he topped his second shot and recorded a double bogey seven, a hard way to start a tournament. He was beginning to wonder if he had made the right decision in playing, but he soon recovered, shooting 73.

During the second day of play, a driving rain storm took place and suspended play twice, Wood, who was three over par at the time and very uncomfortable with his rain-soaked corset and harness, was ready to call it quits. When the rain stopped and play resumed, Tommy Armour, his playing partner, persuaded Wood to continue. Although he bogeyed the next hole, he patiently played on and, despite his ailing back, prevailed and shot 70.

*"In the Rough" 1941 U.S. Open*

*Craig Wood Sinking 30 Foot Putt on 18th Green, Colonial Country Club, Fort Worth, Texas, to win 45th U.S. Open Championship.*

The third day, with 36 holes to play and temperatures in the 90's, Wood shot 70 for par in the morning round and another 70 in the afternoon, finishing with a birdie on the 18th hole. It was an incredible performance and finally he was a champion long overdue.

He had triumphantly weathered the Texas heat and rain with a braced and laced bad back for a three-stroke victory over Densmore Shute and a five-stroke victory over hometown favorite, Ben Hogan. He was now the United States Open Champion.

A.P. Photo

*Craig Wood, the golfer who until this year had been known as the great runner-up, today is the proud possessor of the biggest prize of them all, the U.S.G.A.'s National Open Championship trophy. The 39-year-old veteran from Mamaroneck is seen hugging his prize after winning the title at Fort Worth, Tex.*

Craig Wood, at 39 years of age, had become the oldest American at the time to win the Open and also the first to win the Masters and the Open the same year. He felt that the extreme caution while playing with the bad back, however, had something to do with winning the tournament. He also said that all his life he had wanted to come to the last hole and be able to take three putts to win. He had served notice that he was now the "Number One Wood," having gone from runner up to that of champion.

It was said that Wood lost little time spending the $1,000. The first $100 went for a United States Savings Bond and the next $200 went to his caddy, who had picked him to win. When Wood handed the check to the caddy, the young man took one look at the check and yelled, "Wow! Call me a taxi."

## 1941
## FORTY-FIFTH OPEN CHAMPIONSHIP

Held at the Colonial Club, Fort Worth, Texas, June 5–7.
Yardage—7,005.   Par—70.

1,048 Entries; 163 Starters.
57 Contestants who completed 72 holes.

| | | | | | | Score | Money Prize |
|---|---|---|---|---|---|---|---|
| 1 | Craig Wood, Winged Foot G.C., N.Y. | 73 | 71 | 70 | 70 | 284 | $1,000,00 |
| 2 | Denny Shute, Chicago, Ill. | 69 | 75 | 72 | 71 | 287 | 800.00 |
| 3 | Johnny Bulla, Chicago, Ill. | 75 | 71 | 72 | 71 | 289 | 650.00 |
| | Ben Hogan, Hershey C.C., Pa. | 74 | 77 | 68 | 70 | 289 | 650.00 |
| 5 | Herman Barron, Fenway G.C., N.Y. | 75 | 71 | 74 | 71 | 291 | 412.50 |
| | Paul Runyan, Metropolis C.C., N.Y. | 73 | 72 | 71 | 75 | 291 | 412.50 |
| 7 | E.J. (Dutch) Harrison, Chicago, Ill. | 70 | 82 | 71 | 71 | 294 | 216.67 |
| | Harold L. McSpaden, Winchester C.C., Mass. | 71 | 75 | 74 | 74 | 294 | 216.67 |
| | Gene Sarazen, Lakeview C.C., N.Y. | 74 | 73 | 72 | 75 | 294 | 216.67 |
| 10 | Ed Dudley, Broadmoor G.C., Colo. | 74 | 74 | 74 | 73 | 295 | 125.00 |
| | Lloyd Mangrum, Monterey Park, Calif. | 73 | 74 | 72 | 76 | 295 | 125.00 |
| | Dick Metz, Oak Park,C.C., Ill. | 71 | 74 | 76 | 74 | 295 | 125.00 |
| 13 | Henry Ransom, Glen Garden G. & C.C., Texas | 72 | 74 | 75 | 75 | 296 | 100.00 |
| | Horton Smith, Pinehurst C.C., N.C. | 73 | 75 | 73 | 75 | 296 | 100.00 |
| | Sam Snead, Hot Springs, Va. | 76 | 70 | 77 | 73 | 296 | 100.00 |
| | *Harry Todd, Lakewood C.C., Texas | 72 | 77 | 76 | 71 | 296 | —— |
| 17 | Lawson Little, Monterey Peninsula, Calif. | 71 | 73 | 79 | 74 | 297 | 50.00 |
| | Byron Nelson, Inverness C., Ohio | 73 | 73 | 74 | 77 | 297 | 50.00 |
| 19 | Victor Ghezzi, Deal G.C., N.J. | 70 | 79 | 77 | 72 | 298 | 50.00 |
| 20 | Gene Kunes, Holmesbury C.C., Pa. | 71 | 79 | 74 | 75 | 299 | 50.00 |
| 21 | Ralph Guldahl, Chicago, Ill. | 79 | 76 | 72 | 73 | 300 | 50.00 |
| | Clayton Heafner, Linville G. & C.C., N.C. | 72 | 72 | 78 | 78 | 300 | 50.00 |
| | Johnny Palmer, Badin, N.C. | 74 | 76 | 76 | 74 | 300 | 50.00 |
| 24 | Jimmy Hines, Lakeville C., N.Y. | 75 | 74 | 76 | 76 | 301 | 50.00 |
| 25 | Joseph Zarhardt, Jeffersonville G.C., Pa. | 74 | 76 | 77 | 75 | 302 | 50.00 |
| 26 | Sam Byrd, Merion Cricket C., Pa. | 76 | 78 | 75 | 74 | 303 | 50.00 |
| | Herman Keiser, Firestone C.C., Ohio | 74 | 77 | 76 | 76 | 303 | 50.00 |
| | Johnny Morris, Tuscaloosa C.C., Ala. | 72 | 73 | 81 | 77 | 303 | 50.00 |
| | Henry G. Picard, Twin Hills G. & C.C., Okla. | 77 | 79 | 72 | 75 | 303 | 50.00 |
| 30 | Jim Ferrier, Elmhurst C.C., Ill. | 77 | 71 | 81 | 75 | 304 | 50.00 |
| | Jerry Gianferante, Brattleboro C.C., Vt. | 76 | 77 | 74 | 77 | 304 | 50.00 |
| | *Marvin H. (Bud) Ward, Spokane G.& C.C., Wash. | 76 | 77 | 75 | 76 | 304 | —— |
| 33 | Abe G. Espinosa, C.C. of Decatur, Ill. | 76 | 75 | 72 | 82 | 305 | |
| | Sam Parks, Jr., South Hills C.C., Pa. | 73 | 82 | 74 | 76 | 305 | |
| | Toney Penna, Dayton, Ohio | 75 | 77 | 76 | 77 | 305 | |
| | Marvin D. Stahl, C.C. of Lansing, Mich. | 77 | 76 | 73 | 79 | 305 | |
| | Jimmy Turnesa, Elmsford C.C., N.Y. | 74 | 80 | 77 | 74 | 305 | |
| 38 | Bill Kaiser, Louisville, Ky. | 72 | 78 | 80 | 76 | 306 | |
| 39 | Willie Klein, Wheatley Hills G.C., N.Y. | 73 | 80 | 78 | 76 | 307 | |
| 40 | Bunny Torpey, Oakwood C.C., Mo. | 72 | 79 | 78 | 79 | 308 | |
| | *William P. Turnesa, Meadowbrook C.C., Mich. | 75 | 77 | 75 | 81 | 308 | |
| 42 | Jim Foulis, Ruth Lake C.C., Ill. | 78 | 78 | 74 | 79 | 309 | |
| | Felix Serafin, C.C. of Scranton, Pa. | 76 | 79 | 78 | 76 | 309 | |
| | Mike Turnesa, Fairview C.C., N.Y. | 77 | 79 | 75 | 78 | 309 | |
| 45 | Henry Castillo, L.S.U. G.C., La. | 84 | 72 | 77 | 77 | 310 | |
| | Charles B. Farlow, Piedmont, C.C., N.C. | 79 | 77 | 77 | 77 | 310 | |
| | Bob Hamilton, Helfrich Field G.C., Ind. | 76 | 79 | 80 | 75 | 310 | |
| | Jack Ryan, Louisville C.C., Ky. | 71 | 82 | 80 | 77 | 310 | |
| 49 | *Richard D. Chapman, Winged Foot G.C., N.Y. | 76 | 76 | 80 | 80 | 312 | |
| | Pat Wilcox, Sunnyside C.C., Iowa | 80 | 75 | 79 | 78 | 312 | |
| 51 | Raymond Gafford, Ridglea G.C., Texas | 76 | 78 | 82 | 77 | 313 | |
| 52 | Al Watrous, Oakland Hills C.C., Mich. | 79 | 75 | 81 | 79 | 314 | |
| 53 | Bill Nary, Rancho Santa Fe G.C., Calif. | 77 | 76 | 83 | 79 | 315 | |
| 54 | *John J. Jacobs, III, Cedar Rapids C.C., Iowa | 74 | 77 | 82 | 83 | 316 | |
| 55 | *Verne Stewart, Carrizozo C.C., N.M. | 76 | 78 | 80 | 83 | 317 | |
| 56 | Tom O'Connor, Yardley C.C., Pa. | 73 | 78 | 79 | 88 | 318 | |
| 57 | Jock Hutchison, Jr., Rockford, Ill. | 78 | 78 | 83 | 80 | 319 | |

*Amateur.
Prize money totaling $6,000 awarded to professionals returning scores up to 304, inclusive.

75

# Hale America Tour

With the outbreak of World War II, many tournaments were cancelled, some courses were closed, and golf equipment was just not being produced. Golf, and especially tournament golf, was to take a back seat to the war efforts.

In 1942 the United States Golf Association cancelled the United States Open. Most tournaments that were held had prize offerings of war bonds, while exhibitions were held at service hospitality centers for wounded G.I.'s.

One tournament that was held, however, was the Hale America Open which was played at the Ridgemoor Country Club in Chicago, Illinois. It raised $20,000 in war efforts for Navy Relief and United Services Organizations.

The United States Golf Association, the Professional Golfers' Association and the Chicago District Golf Association sponsored the tournament which was similar to a United States Open, with more than 1,500 golfers, who tried qualifying at twelve different sites around the country.

Although Craig Wood was the 1941 defending Open champion, the 1942 tournament would not be recognized as an official United States Open so Wood held the title of U.S. Open Champion until the war was over.

*Craig Wood walking with Bobby Jones*

In the Hale America tournament, Wood finished in 12th place with rounds of 72, 71, 68 and 72. Wood, who had earlier been slated to become an officer in the Marine Corps was, in the end, rejected because of his bad back.

The patriotic Bobby Jones, then a captain in the Army, who had been retired from competition golf for a few years, played in his last national event, finishing nineteen strokes behind the winner, Ben Hogan.

Hogan, who won the tournament shooting 72, 62, 69 and 68, finished seventeen under par. Besides his victory and war savings bond, he received a medal just like the ones he would later win in forthcoming Opens. Though the 1942 Hale America Open was not officially recognized by the United States Golf Association, professionals participated in the tournament because of patriotic interests.

*Many fans from the Armed Services at the Miami Open*

Craig Wood autographs a scorecard for Seaman Roland Larue of Potsdam, New York, after taking an early lead with a two under par-68 at the 1943 Miami Open.

## 1942
## HALE AMERICA NATIONAL OPEN GOLF TOURNAMENT

for benefit of
Navy Relief Society and United Service Organizations
sponsored by
United States Golf Association
Chicago District Golf Association    Professional Golfers' Assn. of America

Held at the Ridgemoor Country Club, Chicago, Ill., June 18 to 21, inclusive
Yardage—6,519.    Par—72.

1,540 Entries, 107 Qualifiers, 96 Starters
(Local qualifying rounds, 36 holes, May 24-25 at 69 locations. Sectional qualifying
rounds, 54 holes except where noted otherwise, May 26 at Toronto (36 holes);
June 5 at Boston (36 holes); June 5-6 at Chicago, Kansas City, Bloomfield,
N. J.; June 6-7 at Denver, Atlanta, Detroit, Minneapolis, Buffalo,
Cincinnati, Tulsa, Dallas; June 8-9 at Los Angeles.)

All qualifiers eligible for all four rounds. The 62 lowest scorers:

| | | | | | | |
|---|---|---|---|---|---|---|
| 1 | Ben Hogan, Hershey C. C., Pa. | 72 | 62 | 69 | 68 | 271 |
| 2 | Jimmy Demaret, Plum Hollow G. C., Mich. | 68 | 68 | 69 | 69 | 274 |
| | Mike Turnesa, Elmsford C. C., N. Y. | 65 | 66 | 72 | 71 | 274 |
| 4 | Byron Nelson, Inverness C., Ohio | 69 | 70 | 69 | 70 | 278 |
| | Horton Smith, Pinehurst C. C., N.C. | 68 | 67 | 71 | 72 | 278 |
| | Jimmy Thomson, Del Monte G. & C. C., Cal. | 73 | 69 | 70 | 66 | 278 |
| 7 | Eddie Burke, Meadow Brook C. C., Conn. | 71 | 72 | 69 | 68 | 280 |
| | Lawson Little, Monterey, Cal. | 67 | 68 | 71 | 74 | 280 |
| 9 | Jim Ferrier, Elmhurst C. C., Ill. | 69 | 71 | 68 | 73 | 281 |
| | Lloyd Mangrum, Monterey Park, Cal. | 67 | 72 | 71 | 71 | 281 |
| | Dick Metz, Oak Park C. C., Ill. | 68 | 70 | 73 | 70 | 281 |
| 12 | Sam Byrd, Merion G. C., Pa. | 72 | 68 | 71 | 72 | 283 |
| | Harold McSpaden, Philadelphia Country C., Pa. | 71 | 67 | 71 | 74 | 283 |
| | Craig Wood, Winged Foot G. C., N.Y. | 72 | 71 | 68 | 72 | 283 |
| 15 | Herman Barron, Fenway G. C., N.Y. | 68 | 68 | 76 | 72 | 284 |
| | Buck White, Ridgeway C. C., Tenn. | 70 | 69 | 71 | 74 | 284 |
| 17 | Ky Laffoon, Chicago, Ill. | 69 | 70 | 74 | 72 | 285 |
| 18 | Al Brosch, Bethpage Park, N.Y. | 67 | 73 | 70 | 76 | 286 |
| | Toney Penna, Dayton, Ohio | 71 | 72 | 70 | 73 | 286 |
| 20 | Frank Commisso, Irondequoit C. C., N.Y. | 69 | 73 | 71 | 74 | 287 |
| | †John W. Dawson, Lakeside G. C. of Hollywood, Cal. | 71 | 67 | 74 | 75 | 287 |
| | Ed Dudley, Broadmoor G. C., Colo. | 69 | 73 | 71 | 74 | 287 |
| 23 | *Frank Connolly, Lakepointe C. C., Mich. | 72 | 70 | 72 | 74 | 288 |
| | Harry Cooper, Golden Valley G. C., Minn. | 67 | 73 | 71 | 77 | 288 |
| | *Steve Kovach, Brackenridge Heights, C. C., Pa. | 71 | 70 | 73 | 74 | 288 |
| | Ray Mangrum, New York, N.Y. | 70 | 70 | 71 | 77 | 288 |
| | Jack Mitchell, Spring Brook C. C., N.J. | 70 | 71 | 74 | 73 | 288 |
| | Paul Runyan, Metropolis C. C., N.Y. | 72 | 71 | 71 | 74 | 288 |
| 29 | Otey Crisman, Riverside G. C., Ala. | 65 | 72 | 76 | 76 | 289 |
| | *William Y. Dear, Jr., Essex County C. C., N.J. | 72 | 66 | 76 | 75 | 289 |
| | Joe Kirkwood, Huntingdon Valley C. C., Pa. | 70 | 72 | 75 | 72 | 289 |
| | Johnny Morris, Tuscaloosa C. C., Ala. | 71 | 73 | 74 | 71 | 289 |
| | Gene Sarazen, Brooklawn C. C., Conn. | 70 | 72 | 73 | 74 | 289 |
| | George Schneiter, Ogden G. and C. C., Utah | 68 | 73 | 74 | 74 | 289 |
| 35 | Willie Goggin, Century C. C., N.Y. | 69 | 71 | 75 | 75 | 290 |
| | Capt. Robert T. Jones, Jr., Atlanta A. C., Ga. | 70 | 75 | 72 | 73 | 290 |
| | Gib Sellers, Edgewood G. C., Mich. | 70 | 70 | 75 | 75 | 290 |
| | Mike Sipula, Ottawa C. C., Ill. | 67 | 70 | 78 | 75 | 290 |
| | Joe Turnesa, Rockville C. C., N.Y. | 71 | 72 | 73 | 74 | 290 |
| 40 | Abe G. Espinosa, Decatur C. C., Ill. | 69 | 71 | 73 | 78 | 291 |
| | Henry G. Picard, Twin Hills G. & C. C., Okla. | 72 | 73 | 73 | 73 | 291 |
| | Marvin D. Stahl, C. C. of Lansing, Mich. | 69 | 72 | 73 | 77 | 291 |
| 43 | *Robert Cochran, Norwood Hills C. C., Mo. | 69 | 72 | 73 | 78 | 292 |
| | Joe Coria, Phalen G. C., Minn. | 70 | 72 | 76 | 74 | 292 |
| | *Neil Croonquist, The C. C., Minneapolis, Minn. | 72 | 70 | 76 | 74 | 292 |
| | John Krutilla, Burnham Woods C. C., Ill. | 72 | 73 | 72 | 75 | 292 |
| | Denny Shute, Chicago, Ill. | 69 | 68 | 80 | 75 | 292 |
| | *Frank Stranahan, Miami Biltmore C. C., Fla. | 72 | 71 | 74 | 75 | 292 |
| | Sgt. Jim Turnesa, Fort Dix, N.J. | 71 | 72 | 73 | 76 | 292 |
| 50 | Dick Govern, Skaneateles C. C., N.Y. | 73 | 72 | 74 | 74 | 293 |
| | Ralph Guldahl, Chicago, Ill. | 73 | 71 | 78 | 71 | 293 |
| | Al Huske, Kishwaukee C. C., Ill. | 71 | 74 | 73 | 75 | 293 |
| 53 | Harry Adams, Medina C. C., Ill. | 72 | 77 | 72 | 73 | 294 |
| | John Kinder, Plainfield C. C., N.J. | 72 | 72 | 74 | 76 | 294 |
| | Herman Scharlau, Bloomington C. C., Ill. | 79 | 70 | 75 | 70 | 294 |
| 56 | Joe Belfore, C. C. of Detroit, Mich. | 71 | 74 | 76 | 74 | 295 |
| | Raymond Gafford, Ridglea G. C., Texas | 70 | 74 | 74 | 77 | 295 |
| | James S. Johnson, Warren Valley G. C., Mich. | 71 | 73 | 76 | 75 | 295 |
| | Frank Moore, St. Clair C. C., Ill. | 71 | 74 | 74 | 76 | 295 |
| | Tom Talbot, Columbia C. C., Mo. | 71 | 71 | 79 | 74 | 295 |
| | *Wilford Wehrle, Racine, Wis. | 68 | 70 | 76 | 81 | 295 |
| | *Neil E. White, Tamarack C. C., Conn. | 72 | 73 | 76 | 74 | 295 |

*Amateurs. †Applicant for reinstatement to amateur classification.
Prize money totaling $6,000 awarded to professionals returning scores up to 289, inclusive; $1,200 of total in War Savings Bonds.
"Old Guard" Division—for players who competed in USGA Open Championships at least 20 years ago—won by Ed Dudley, 287.

# Ryder Cup

The Ryder Cup matches were started in 1927 by a businessman named Samuel Ryder. Ryder felt that the matches between America and Great Britain would foster good will between the two countries as well as some good head-to-head competition, not to mention the socialization it would provide.

The first official matches were held in 1927 at the Worcester Golf Club in Massachusetts, where the Americans, under Captain Walter Hagen, captured the trophy 9½-2 ½.

Wood played on the 1931 team and won his single match played at the Scioto, Ohio course, defeating Arthur Havers four down with three to go. The United States won easily, showing their supremacy.

In 1933 the United States team, on which Wood was a member, gathered in New York City before sailing to Great Britain for one of the most famous and exciting matches ever played.

Wood was victorious in his singles match at Southport, England, defeating W.H. Davies by a match score of 4 and 3. J.H. Taylor, captain of the British team, had his men running on the beaches early every morning as well as other forms of physical activity which paid off. They were successful in winning the cup and it would be 24 years before Great Britain would win again.

In 1935 the matches were played at the Ridgewood Country Club in New Jersey again under Walter Hagen's captaincy. Craig Wood was named as a co-captain and, although the United States team won, Wood lost his singles match to Percy Allis after being three up before lunch.

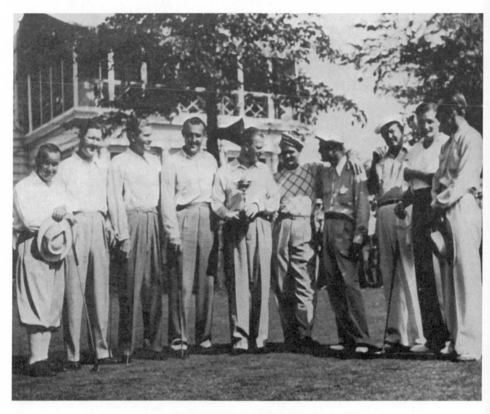

*Ryder Cup American Team*

In 1941 the competition was cancelled because of the war. Wood was a member and captain of the team, although there were no matches held.

*Ryder Cup American Team*

In 1947 the matches resumed in Portland, Oregon. Wood and Walter Hagen were the honorary captains. The American team won the first eleven matches - the biggest victory margin in the history of the matches.

In 1979 the event was expanded to its present day format, which includes non-British Europeans and has continued to grow into a very great and popular international competition.

# Winged Foot Golf Club

From 1940-1946 Wood held the esteemed position of head professional at the famed and exclusive Winged Foot Golf Club in Mamaroneck, New York.

Those were some of his greatest years and fondest memories, for he loved working there and the members loved having him as their professional.

Winged Foot Archives

*Clubhouse at Winged Foot in Mamaroneck, New York designed by master architect, A.W. Tillinghast. A great test of golf, having held many major tournaments.*

The members felt great pride in their well-dressed professional who had captured The Masters and United States Open, while employed at Winged Foot. There were many large congratulatory celebrations and jubilant parties held for him in New York City upon his return.

While at Winged Foot he would play as much golf as he possibly could with the members and very often he would walk through the locker room and yell out "does anyone need a game today?" He treated everyone the same, just like a family and they responded in turn.

There was a definite aura of class and sophistication about Craig Wood. He was extremely polished not only in his playing ability and overall good manners but polished also as a good business man. He and his assistants gave more lessons, sold more clubs, made more money than any other club professionals throughout the country. One story that is told about Wood was that while most pros took financial advice from the members, the members more often sought out Wood for financial advice.

In 1944 while playing occasionally, for he was semi-retired in terms of competitive golf, he staged one of his greatest comebacks at the Durham Open shooting 67, 67, 67, and 68 to win the tournament.

Before he retired in 1946 he helped a longtime friend of his named Claude Harmon, from Savannah, Georgia to become his successor. Harmon, who would win the Masters in 1948, was widely regarded by his peers for his teaching skills as well as his playing ability.

Harmon thought so much of his friend Craig Wood that he named one of his own sons after him. Craig Harmon is the head professional at Oak Hill Country Club in Rochester, New York. The other Harmon boys - Dick, Butch and Bill, all respected players and teachers themselves, grew up calling Craig Wood, "Uncle Craig" because there was such a great deal of love and respect in the Harmon family for him.

After 1946 when he left Winged Foot, Wood opened Ford Dealerships in New York and New Jersey. Henry Ford, a member of Winged Foot and a friend of his, helped him in the business venture.

In later years Wood often returned to play golf with his many friends at his beloved Winged Foot course. On his 66th birthday, after not having played in competition for close to twenty years, he shot 66 on the West Course.

*Craig Wood of Winged Foot holding trophy after winning The*
*U.S. Open in 1941. He would hold the title for five years,*
*since the tournament wasn't held again til after World War II.*

# Dunlop

In the 1930's Wood represented the Dunlop Tire and Rubber Company and worked in their equipment development department.

The well-educated Wood became an executive and was a great asset to the company, especially for his discovery and signing of a number of talented young professionals whom he had met while playing tournament golf.

Over the years he helped many young pros in the early years of their careers, such as Dick Metz, Mike Souchak, Claude Harmon, Vic Ghezzi and Sam Snead.

He told the young Snead, while playing a tournament in the Bahamas, that if he had a hard time meeting expenses on the west coast to call him and he would help.

He also signed the twenty-four year old Snead to a contract with Dunlop for his endorsement. Wood was certainly correct in his assessment of the talented Snead, for he would go on to win 135 tournaments all over the world and needless to say never had to call Wood for any help.

Johnny Bulla, who was a runner up in the 1939 British Open said *"Wood not only helped the struggling pros coming up, but he even paid attention to the caddies, whereas many of the other professionals would never take the time."*

*The Dunlop golf ball that Craig Wood used displaying his name.*

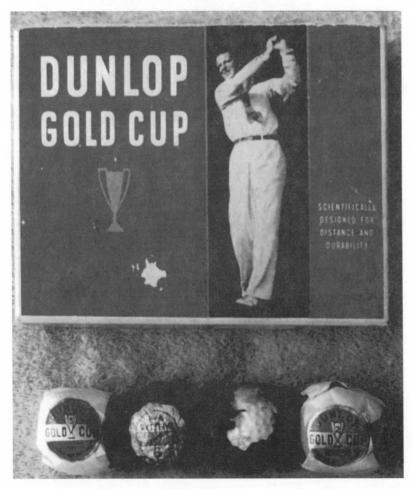

## *How to use the driver* by Craig Wood

With the Vardon grip, the club is placed in the palm of the left hand, so that the first three knuckles of the hand are visible. The club is then placed in the fingers of the right hand so that the little finger overlaps the fore-finger of the left hand. The points of the V shapes should be parallel and point to the right shoulder.

The square distance is recommended for all types of wood-play. This means that feet should be parallel to line of desired flight. The ball should be in line with the left heel. Foot-spread should be slightly wider than width of shoulders. Hands should be low and close to body, right shoulder down, hips and legs relaxed, weight evenly distributed.

The same action of the back-swing also applies to all wood-clubs. The club-head is started back with a straight left arm, with the left hand firmly in control. There is a gradual shifting of the weight to the right as the club is started up with a slow even stroke. The hips pivot from left to right. At the top of the swing the left knee bends toward the right, with the right hip well back. The weight at this point is on the right foot, with the left heel slightly off the ground. The left arm is slightly bent at the top, left shoulder is pointed toward the ball, and club-shaft is parallel with ground.

The start of the downward swing is a smooth, slow pull of the left arm, with the wrists cocked and the left arm almost rigidly straight. With the swing, the weight shifts evenly to the left side, the left heel again becomes set as the right heel gradually rises off the ground.

Just before the amount of impact, the right hand and right arm begin to take charge of the swing and wrists uncock. The right shoulder is now down, the left arm straight, and the right arm slightly bent. The right heel at this point is well off the ground, the hips ahead of address position, and the left side braced against a straight left leg as the ball is hit.

The body and weight now begin to move forward
and to the left, as the head turns toward the objective.
The left leg is still braced with the right foot moving up on
the toe. The right shoulder is low. Arms are relaxed. The
follow

through continues with right arm
straight, and right knee bent. The body
pivots around fully to face the direction
of flight. The weight stays firmly on the
left foot. Finish freely on right toe to
allow complete body-turn.

# Lake Placid Exhibition

*Lake Placid Golf and Country Club*

In 1924 local businessmen and the Lake Placid Chamber of Commerce purchased the Alfred Peck Farms located on the road to the Cascade Lakes. Twenty five persons then formed the Lake Placid Holding Company and named the nine-hole course, designed by Seymour Dunn, the Lake Placid Golf and Country Club.

The layout had unusual significance for Craig Wood, because the farm had been an old homestead where his grandfather had grown up.

The course officially opened in 1925 as a nine-hole course and was lengthened to eighteen holes in 1932 with John Van Kleek as the architect.

*Craig Wood Golf Course*

*Len Tyrell, the first club professional, practicing his swing.*

As you can see, winter in Lake Placid can be quite long.

Craig Wood of Rumson, N. J., a strong contender for the money in Lake Placid Open, got early start in golfing career in this village.

# CRAIG WOOD TO PLAY EXHIBITION MATCH AT LAKE PLACID COUNTRY CLUB OPENING WEDNESDAY

## Brothers to Play Against Brothers, Wood and Brother to Meet Tyrell Pros. Marking Opening of New Nine Holes

Craig Wood of Deal, N. J., has accepted the invitation issued by the North Elba Park commission to play an exhibition match here Wednesday to mark the opening of the new nine holes of the Lake Placid Golf and Country club to the public.

Wood, who was runner up in the British open last month and has placed well up in all of the western and southern tournaments last winter will play in an exhibition foursome with his brother, Scott Wood of this village as partner. They will oppose R. A. "Hike" Tyrell, pro at Meadowbrook course, Saranac Lake, and his brother, L. J. Tyrell, Lake Placid Golf club professional. Mr. Wood is the son of Mr. and Mrs. Charles Wood of this village. Receiving his early training by carrying clubs and watching the mistakes of others, he has been climbing steadily in his profession, nearly reaching the top when he was defeated at St. Andrews, Scotland, by Densmore Shute. The match of paired brothers is to be open to the public without charge as a part of the ceremonies of the opening of the course.

Aug. 28, 1936

# Official Opening
## Second Nine Holes
### Lake Placid Golf and Country Club
# Wednesday, Aug. 9 Two P.M.

---

## ATTRACTION EXTRAORDINARY!!

---

Craig Wood, Runner-up for British Open Championship, in Exhibition 18-hole Match

With Three Other Star Products of Lake Placid Courses

## The Four - Brother Foursome
### [FIRST TIME IN GOLF HISTORY]

### Craig Wood
Lake Placid boy, pro. at Deal, N. J., runner-up in
British Open, and high money winner in 1933
Winter Tourneys.

— AND —

### Scott Wood
Lake Placid Golf and Country Club Amateur Star

### L. J. (Dick) Tyrell
Pro. at Lake Placid Golf and Country Club

**VS.**

— AND —

### R. A. (Hike) Tyrell
Pro. at Meadowbrook Golf Club, Saranac Lake

## Admission Free

Come and See This Famous Match on the Most Beautiful 18-hole Scenic Lay-out in
the Adirondacks

---

## Lake Placid Golf and Country Club
### [18-HOLE CHAMPIONSHIP COURSE]

15-minute Drive from Lake Placid on New Macadam Cascade Highway

100

In 1933, the Lake Placid Country Club's 18 holes were opened with the Tyrell brothers and the Wood brothers playing the first round. The picture was taken as they teed off before a large group of admirers. From left, Len Tyrell, his brother Hike, Craig Wood and his brother Scott.

Hike Tyrell and Craig Wood, childhood friends,
caddies and professionals.

Members of the Lake Placid summer colony
were out in full force to watch the four-brother match
and opening ceremonies, where the Wood brothers
defeated the Tyrell brothers by a margin of seven
strokes. Wood shot 36-34 on the par 73 course.

That afternoon Wood played his second 18-hole
match when he competed in the weekly Adirondack
Amateur and Professional Tournament held at the
Whiteface Inn Golf Club. He played the course in one
under par 70 and but for his misfortune on the 17th
hole, where it took him two shots to get out of the
bunker, he played well enough to win the
tournament. Hike Tyrell was third with a 75.

Hike Tyrell grew up caddying at the Ruisseaumont Golf Course on Riki Hill in Lake Placid the same time as did Wood. Tyrell was the pro at the Ray Brook Course (known then as the Meadowbrook Course) for sixty years. He was a great player and renowned teacher who helped many of his fellow professionals such as Willie Goggin and Ben Hogan.

Hogan spent a summer in Lake Placid and worked on his swing with Tyrell. He was fighting an uncontrollable hook at the time and it was said that by the time Tyrell opened the shop in the morning, Hogan had already hit hundreds of balls.

Local boy, Craig Wood,
who became a golfing great
and hall of fame member for
winning the 1941 Masters,
and the U.S. Open. Here
once again he plays
"brothers" vs. "brothers"
with Len and Hike Tyrell
and brother Scott.

# CRAIG WOOD
## EXHIBITION DAY

SEE THE
### U. S. Open Champion
## on the
# Lake Placid
# Golf and
# Country Club
### 18-hole
### Championship Course
## on
# WEDNESDAY
# JULY 23
### at 2 P. M.

## 18 Hole Match
# Craig and Scott Wood
# Hike and Len Tyrell

*Proceeds Benefit*
*Kiwanis and Lions Club Children's Work*

*Sponsors Ticket $1* on sale Olympic Arena
and Country Club

# CRAIG WOOD

## NATIONAL OPEN CHAMPION

## Will play on the Champlain Course Sunday afternoon - July 27th.

He will pair with Roger Prescott against Chet Taylor and Geo. Gillespie. 3:00 P. M.

A month after winning the United States Open, Wood played in a golf exhibition in Plattsburgh at the Hotel Champlain (Bluff Point) Course.

Wood shot 71, his partner, Roger Prescott shot 79, the Bluff Point pro, Chet Taylor had 73 and his partner, George Gillespie, posted a 74.

*Home town hero*

*On green of 1st hole of Craig Wood course*

*Driving ball in front of friends at the Craig Wood course in
Lake Placid*

In 1948 Craig Wood was honored again by his lifelong friends at the Lake Placid Golf and Country Club by having the course officially named for him. It was a living memorial to the man who brought honor to his home town of Lake Placid. Hundreds attended the July 19 ceremonies and the exhibition.

The exhibition event teamed Wood with Jim Searle, the Director of Golf at the Lake Placid Club (not to be confused with the Lake Placid Golf and Country Club), which had just been changed to the Craig Wood Golf and Country Club. They played against Claude Harmon, the Winged Foot Golf Professional and winner of the 1948 Masters and Marshall Trusttum, the Craig Wood course pro.

Harmon and Trusttum won by a two-up margin after being one down at the turn. Harmon shot 36-31 for 67 while Wood shot 34-33 for another 67. Searle carded a 76 and Trusttum an 81.

*Bobby Locke, Jim Searle, Craig Wood & Claude Harmon*

A week later, while Wood was in Lake Placid, another exhibition match was played at the Lake Placid Club Lower Course. Craig Wood and Claude Harmon took on and defeated Bobby Locke (Canadian Open & South African Open Champion) and Lake Placid Club pro Jim Searle two up with one to go in match play. Wood shot 67 on the par 70 course while his partner reigning Masters Champion Claude Harmon shot 71. Locke shot 68 while Searle shot 73. It was a well-attended exhibition with magnificent shotmaking by all four pros.

Craig Wood, showing his grip to a distinguished group of hometown boys who had accomplished many feats in the world of sports themselves. From left to right, Chet Taylor, P.G.A. Golf Professional, Jack Shea, who won two gold medals in the 1932 Winter Olympics in the 500 and 1500 meters and Stan Benham, who won two silver medals for bobsledding at the 1952 Winter Olympics in Oslo, Norway.

*Showing the Vardon or overlapping grip he used*

In 1964 Arnold Palmer, who had won the United States Open and The Masters in 1960, played an exhibition match at Craig Wood Golf and Country Club with John Doctor, golf pro at the Bluff Point Golf Course in Plattsburgh, New York, Hike Tyrell, golf pro at the Ray Brook Golf Course in Ray Brook, New York and Craig Wood.

In July 1967, Wood was invited by the townspeople to Craig Wood Country Club, where he was given a token of appreciation by the Town of North Elba for his contribution to making the town's name known throughout the world of golf.

# CRAIG WOOD
## 50th ANNIVERSARY
## VICTORY DINNER

Sunday, August 25, 1991

To commemorate Craig Wood's 1941
Victories in the U. S. Open and
Masters Golf Tournaments

*The Craig Wood Golf Association of Lake Placid also held a
golf tournament commemorating him.*

Originally called the Lake Placid Golf and Country Club, the name was changed to Craig Wood to honor its native son.

The Craig Wood Golf Course is today a par 72, 6,554-yard municipal course owned and operated by the Town of North Elba, New York. It was originally a nine-hole course designed by Seymour Dunn in 1925 and lengthened in 1932 by architect John Van Kleek, although Dunn had originally helped in the design.

The course record of 63 is held by Larry Barry of Lake Placid, New York, established July 19, 1998. The previous course record was held by Gene Sarazen.

*The original club house was built in 1925 and remodeled in 1933. It was demolished in the 1980's and replaced with the present club house.*

*The course is a rolling plateau with the majestic peaks of the Ancient Adirondack Mountains on all sides.*

# Indian Lodge Hunting Camp

When Wood was not playing golf, there was no place he would rather be than back home in the mountains spending time with family and friends hunting, fishing and relaxing.

He was a woodsman who was just as tough in the woods as his lumberman father had been. He also showed the same determination when in pursuit of wild game as he had shown on the golf course. There are a few good hunting stories, however, about him worth mentioning.

One time when hunting in the back woods of the Adirondacks, a companion of his shot a deer and the bullet ricocheted off a rock, entering Wood's thigh in fragments. The stoic Wood was unfazed by the accident and continued hunting for the remainder of the day. A week later he played in a golf tournament in the south and was still picking shrapnel out of the wounds.

Another time while hunting on a very cold, raw, below freezing morning, he fell through the ice while crossing a stream. Drenched to the bone from head to toe he struggled through the freezing water, managing to reach the other side and with his powerful legs, crawled to dry land. He then continued hunting for the rest of the day without ever giving a second thought to going back to camp and change into dry and warm clothes.

Wood used to use bits of venison as trout bait.

Kelly Family Photo

*Home on leave, Richard Palumbo, Assistant Golf Pro
at the Lake Placid Country Club
displaying his catch from Lake Placid.*

In his later years, while living in New York City, he was the owner of a 1,200-acre hunting lodge in the Catskill Mountains called Big Indian Lodge. It was his favorite spot to escape the city life.

*Craig Wood, Russell Bigel, President of Montgomery Ward, and Edward Waugh, Winged Foot Golf Club Chairman, at Big Indian Lodge.*

*Hometown friends Jack Shea and Craig Wood*
*relaxing at Big Indian Lodge*

Having won two gold medals in speed skating in the 1932 Olympic Winter Games, Shea, a champion in his own right, greatly admired Wood, whom he considered his friend and confidant. He felt that his life was much enriched by Wood's friendship and company.

*Wood, Shea and friend at hunting camp*

Lawton Carver, who owned and operated a popular east side restaurant in New York City, was a good friend of his and a frequent hunting and fishing companion. Carver said that Wood, who was a true marksman with a rifle, loved his hunting lodge and loved to celebrate with his good friends in seclusion away from the glitter of sports celebrity.

Wood used to buy 100 bushels of apples a month to feed the many deer which grazed on the lodge property. The apples, interestingly enough, were sold to him by Gene Sarazen, who defeated him in the 1934 Masters and who had lived on a farm above the Catskill Mountains.

# Lucaya Resort

In 1961, Wood, who had been semi retired since leaving the Winged Foot Club in 1946, was offered a job he couldn't refuse.

A Navy admiral, who was a close friend of his, had heard of a new position being created in the Grand Bahamas as the Director of Golf at the Lucaya Club in Freeport.

Knowing Wood and also knowing the investment group that owned the club, he knew Craig would be the right front man for the position.

Within the month he was hired and assisted legendary Dick Wilson in the design of the 6,829-yard Lucaya course that was being built.

The course was completed in 1962 and was rated at one time as one of the best 100 golf courses in the world. The island course had punishing doglegs and intense bunkering that demanded accuracy off the tee.

*The Lucaya Golf Course which still honors Craig Wood is now 36 holes and home to the P.G.A. Senior Slam as well as home of Butch Harmon School of Golf.*

*Wood the Goodwill Ambassador*

Wood hadn't played in any major tournament since leaving his Winged Foot position and in those days there was no Senior Tour. He had also chosen not to represent any club because he had made sound financial investments and didn't need to work. However, this position as the Director of Golf in the Bahamas somehow seemed to suit him at this stage of his life.

After the course opened he spent most of his time giving lessons and playing golf with members and resort guests.

He was the classic goodwill ambassador and needless to say was liked and respected by everyone he met.

For the next few years he and his wife, who had
left the social New York City life, fell in love with the
island life and the people.

The champion that he was could still play golf
like the competitor he had once been, shooting a 66
at the Lucaya course.

Tragedy struck him later in that year however,
when his wife Jacqueline passed away. His health
seemed to suffer after that and a year later while
playing with members, he suffered a mild heart attack.

The next day he took a plane to Palm Beach,
Florida for treatment. While in his hotel room he
suffered a severe heart attack and passed away at the
age of 67.

# Back Home & Laid to Rest, Lake Placid

After the large funeral, which was held in New York City, Wood was brought back to Lake Placid and laid to rest in the North Elba Cemetery, not far from where he first learned the game as a young caddy.

Wood had been elected to the Professional Golfers' Association Hall of Fame in 1956, and honored as a man who had made outstanding contributions to the game. As a golfer he had the courage to keep battling through after being second so many times in his career and with perseverance he had emerged from being the perennial runner up to that of champion.

All his fellow professionals cherished his friendship and mourned his departure, for he was both generous and helpful to a great many of them in their early careers.

One professional, P.G.A. champion, Jackie Burke Jr., said of Wood, "*adversity didn't bother him, ailing didn't bother him and he didn't talk about his wounds. He was one hell of a dude, I'll tell you that.*"

Charles Price, the eloquent golf writer, once wrote, "*if there was a popularity contest with the Professional Golfers' Association, he would win by so many votes the tally would look like a zip code.*"

Lawson Carter, who was a close friend and sports editor for the International Paper Service, wrote a requiem for his old camp fire crony after he passed away, remembering Wood as a golfer with great personal class. All of the stories regarding him centered around or touched upon that facet of him and the class that he brought to anything he did, including losing more important close finishes than any player of his time.

When he died last spring many of the stories revived about the big, good-looking, blond-headed slugger centered around or touched upon that other facet of his, the class he brought to anything he did, including losing in more important close finishes than any other player of his time. He lost a playoff for the only British Open he ever entered, lost a PGA championship in extra holes, a Masters in a playoff and the U.S. Open in a double playoff, among several such to enhance for him his big wins in both the Masters and the U.S. Open of 1941.

The only public comment worthy of note that he ever made on his several near misses and the anguish of it came when a reporter asked him if he choked up in the clutch. As quietly well-mannered as ever Craig's reply was that it may take more courage to keep on losing the close ones than to win them.

## Guido Cribari, a writer and friend wrote

The Good Lord has taken the Number One Wood out of professional golf. And the game will never seem the same.

The sudden passing of Craig Wood from America's sports scene has saddened the hearts of golfers from Mamaroneck to Madagascar. For he was loved and admired throughout the world.

He was a super-star of his game. He was universally respected by everyone fortunate enough to have made his acquaintance. He was a pro's pro, a man's man, a gentleman's gentleman.

Craig was laid to rest yesterday among the lovely hills of Lake Placid, whence he came almost a half century ago to eventually dominate his era and stamp his name indelibly in the record books as one of the all-time greats of golf.

Jack Shea, Olympic hero, Town Supervisor and longtime friend of Craig Wood, gave the final tribute to him at his memorial service in Lake Placid.

*"Representing the Town of North Elba and the Village of Lake Placid, New York, this tribute honors Craig Wood our native son who was universally loved, admired and respected by all and will be remembered for the recognition, honor and international fame he has brought to Lake Placid as one of the greatest golfers ever to play the game."*

CRAIG WOOD
*Golf & Country Club*
THIS GOLF COURSE NAMED IN HONOR OF
CRAIG WOOD
*Native son of Lake Placid*
*1941 U.S. Open*
*Masters & Canadian*
*Champion*

*Laid to Rest,*
*Town of North Elba Cemetery*
*on Old Military Road, Lake Placid*
*not far from where he was born.*

November 18, 1901
May 8, 1968

# *Tournament Wins*

## CRAIG WOOD

BORN:     November 18, 1901
BIRTHPLACE:     Lake Placid, New York
TURNED PROFESSIONAL:     1920
CAREER VICTORIES:     21

1928  New Jersey PGA
1929  Oklahoma Open
1929  Hawaiian Open
1930  New Jersey PGA
1930  Oklahoma City Open
1931  Harlingen Open
1932  New Jersey PGA Match Play
1932  San Francisco Open-Match Play
1932  Pasadena Open
1933  Los Angeles Open
1933  Radium Springs Open
1934  Galveston Open Championship
1934  New Jersey Open
1936  General Brock Open
1938  Augusta Open-Forest Hills
1940  Metropolitan Open
1940  Miami-Biltmore Four-Ball
1941  Masters Tournament
1941  U.S. Open Championship
1942  Canadian Open
1944  Durham Open

# Tournament Record

| YEAR BY YEAR: | 1ST | 2ND | 3RD | TOP 10 | TOP 25 |
|---|---|---|---|---|---|
| 1925 | | | | 1 | 4 |
| 1926 | | | | | 1 |
| 1927 | | | | 3 | 4 |
| 1928 | 1 | 1 | 1 | 4 | 7 |
| 1929 | 2 | | 2 | 11 | 17 |
| 1930 | 2 | | 1 | 13 | 15 |
| 1931 | 1 | 1 | | 7 | 11 |
| 1932 | 3 | 2 | 1 | 11 | 15 |
| 1933 | 2 | 2 | 5 | 12 | 15 |
| 1934 | 2 | 5 | | 14 | 15 |
| 1935 | | 2 | | 4 | 10 |
| 1936 | 1 | 3 | 4 | 10 | 15 |
| 1937 | | | | 5 | 11 |
| 1938 | 1 | 2 | | 7 | 8 |
| 1939 | | 3 | | 7 | 8 |
| 1940 | 2 | 1 | 1 | 9 | 14 |
| 1941 | 2 | 3 | 3 | 17 | 20 |
| 1942 | 1 | 1 | | 6 | 8 |
| 1943 | | 1 | | 2 | 2 |
| 1944 | 1 | 1 | 2 | 13 | 14 |
| 1945 | | | | 10 | 11 |
| 1946 | | | | 1 | 2 |
| 1947 | | | | | 1 |
| 1948 | | | | | 1 |
| 1949 | | | | | 2 |
| | 21 | 28 | 20 | 167 | 229 |

# *Glossary*
## *of*
## *Lake Placid Golf Courses*

Lake Placid Club
     Two 18 Hole Courses and Two 9 Hole Courses

Whiteface Inn
     18 Hole Course

Stevens Hotel Golf Course
       (also called the Lake Placid Golf Course)
     9 Hole Course           (Closed)

Ruisseaumont Golf Course
     15 Hole Course         (Closed)

Fawn Club Course
     9 Hole Course          (Closed)

Craig Wood Country Club & Golf Course
       Previously called Lake Placid Country Club
     18 Hole Course

Meadowbrook Golf Course
      aka Ray Brook
     9 Hole Course
          also
**Tri Lakes Courses**
     Saranac Inn          18 Hole Course
     Tupper Lake       18 Hole Course

# Bibliography

## Book Acknowledgments

Sincere appreciation to the golf writers listed below:

Barkow, Al; *Golf's Golden Grind*, Harcourt Brace
Jovanovich, New York & London, 1974.

Graffis, Herb; *The P.G.A.*, Thomas Crowell Co., New York, 1975.

Dunn, John; *ABC of Golf*, Harpers, 1916.

Dunn, Seymour; *Golf Fundamentals*, Saratogian, 1922.

Goodner, Ross; *Golf's Greatest*, Golf Digest, 1978.

Hagen, Walter; *The Walter Hagen Story*,
Simon & Schuster, New York, 1956.

Martin, H.R.; *Fifty Years of American Golf*, Argosy Antiquarian, 1966.

Martin, J. Peter; *Adirondack Golf Courses Past & Present*,
Adirondack Golf, Lake Placid, 1987.

Winch, Oliver; *Wilmington of the Adirondacks*, 2nd Edition, 1974.

Wind, Herbert Warren; *The Story of American Golf*,
Alfred A. Knopf, New York, 1975.

Wind, Herbert Warren; *The Complete Golfer*,
Simon & Schuster, New York, 1954.

U.S.G.A. Record Book 1895 - 1954, Farhills, New Jersey.


## Magazine Articles Acknowledgments

Carver, Lawton; The Number One Wood, Professional
Golfer, August 1968, page 18

Labbance, Bob; Historical Perspective Wood's
Silver Slam, New York Golf, 1997, page 63 - 66

Miller, Richard; The Triumph of Craig Wood, Golf
Journal, June 1991, page 32

Moriarty, Jim; Due Diligence, Golf World,
June 2001, page 70 - 73

Price, Charles; Lucaya: For The Discerning Golfer,
Golf Magazine, May 1968, page 16

Price, Charles; He Knew Where Golf Was Going,
Golf Magazine, January 1981, page 24

VanSickle, Gary; The Short Heard Round The World,
Golf World, 1995, Vintage Issue.

Whitten, Ron; Another Opinion, Golf World,
March 2000, page 60 - 62.

Whitten, Ron, Double Vision, Golf World,
March 2000, page 60 - 62.